What People Are Saying about Threshold Bible Study

"Stephen Binz's Threshold Bible Study is a marvelous project. With lucidity and creativity, Binz offers today's believing communities a rich and accessible treasury of biblical scholarship. The series' brilliance lies in its simplicity of presentation complemented by critical depth of thought and reflective insight. This is a wonderful gift for personal and communal study, especially for those wishing to make a home for the Word in their hearts."

Carol J. Dempsey, OP, Associate Professor of Theology,
University of Portland, Oregon

"Threshold Bible Study accurately describes this user-friendly series that is aimed at anyone interested in a serious study of the Bible whether alone or in a group. Written in a sprightly easy-to-understand style, these volumes will engage the mind, heart, and spirit of the reader who utilizes the helpful resources author Stephen J. Binz makes available."

Alexander A. Di Lella, OFM, Andrews-Kelly-Ryan Professor of Biblical Studies,
The Catholic University of America

"In an increasingly Bible-reading and Bible-praying Church these helpful books combine solid biblical information and challenging suggestions for personal and group prayer. By covering a wide variety of themes and topics they continually breathe new life into ancient texts."

John R. Donahue, SJ,
Raymond E. Brown Professor Emeritus of New Testament Studies,
St. Mary's Seminary and University, Baltimore, Maryland

"Threshold Bible Study successfully bridges the painful gap between solid biblical scholarship and the rich spiritual nourishment that we expect to find in the words of Scripture. In this way, indispensable biblical knowledge leads to that spiritual wisdom which enables us to live in accord with God's purposes. Stephen Binz is to be congratulated for responding to this urgent need in today's world."

Demetrius Dumm, OSB,
Professor of New Testament, Saint Vincent Seminary,
Saint Vincent Archabbey, Latrobe, Pennsylvania

"Threshold Bible Study offers a marvelous new : to study themes in our rich biblical and theologica e-matic units feels like gazing at panels of stained es through different lights."

Jesuit Schoc. ey

"Threshold Bible Study provides an introduction to some major biblical themes, enabling Catholics to read, with greater understanding, the Bible in the Church. When studied along with the documents of Vatican II and the *Catechism of the Catholic Church*, this series can be a help for personal and group Bible study."

Francis Cardinal George, OMI, Archbishop of Chicago

"The Church has called Scripture a 'font' and 'wellspring' for the spiritual life. Threshold Bible Study is one of the best sources for tapping into the biblical font. Pope John Paul II has stressed that 'listening to the Word of God should become a life-giving encounter.' This is precisely what Threshold Bible Study offers to you—an encounter with the Word that will make your heart come alive." Tim Gray, President of the Augustine Institute, Professor of Sacred Scripture at St. John Vianney Theological Seminary

"Threshold Bible Study is the perfect series of Bible study books for serious students with limited time. Each lesson is brief, illuminating, challenging, wittily written, and a pleasure to study. The reader will reap a rich harvest of wisdom from the efforts expended."

John J. Pilch, Adjunct Professor of Biblical Studies, Georgetown University, Washington, DC

"Threshold Bible Study is an enriching and enlightening approach to understanding the rich faith which the Scriptures hold for us today. Written in a clear and concise style, Threshold Bible Study presents solid contemporary biblical scholarship, offers questions for reflection and/or discussion, and then demonstrates a way to pray from the Scriptures. All these elements work together to offer the reader a wonderful insight into how the sacred texts of our faith can touch our lives in a profound and practical way today. I heartily recommend this series to both individuals and to Bible study groups."

Abbot Gregory J. Polan, OSB, Conception Abbey and Seminary College

"Stephen Binz has put together a great aid in one of the most important aspects of Catholic Christian life today: Bible study. Largely the purview for non-Catholic Christian laity in the past, recent years have seen Catholics hungering for Scripture study and application in their daily lives. Stephen Binz's series promises to help meet that need."

John Michael Talbot, Catholic Christian recording artist, Founder of The Brothers and Sisters of Charity at Little Portion Hermitage

"Threshold Bible Study is that rare kind of program that will help one cross an elusive threshold—using the Bible effectively for prayer and spiritual enrichment. This user-friendly program will enhance any personal or group Bible study. Guaranteed to make your love of Scripture grow!" Ronald D. Witherup, SS, biblical scholar, educator, author, and Superior General of the Sulpician Order

THRESHOLD
BIBLE STUDY

JESUS,
the SUFFERING
SERVANT

PART TWO

Mark
[9–16]

STEPHEN J. BINZ

TWENTY
THIRD *23rd*
PUBLICATIONS
NEW LONDON, CT 06320

SECOND PRINTING 2016

TWENTY-THIRD PUBLICATIONS
A Division of Bayard
One Montauk Avenue, Suite 200
New London, CT 06320
(860) 437-3012 or (800) 321-0411
www.23rdpublications.com

    Library of Congress Cataloging-in-Publication Data
Binz, Stephen J., 1955-
 Jesus, the suffering servant. Part two, Mark 9-16 / Stephen J. Binz.
    pages cm. — (Threshold Bible study)
  ISBN 978-1-58595-864-1
1. Bible. N.T. Mark, IX-XVI—Textbooks. 2. Christian education—Textbooks for adults.
I. Title. II. Title: Mark 9-16.
  BS2585.55.B57 2012
  226.30071—dc23
                        2011049664

ISBN 978-1-58595-864-1
Printed in the U.S.A.

Contents

LESSONS 13–18

LESSONS 19–24

LESSONS 25–30

How to Use
Threshold Bible Study

Threshold Bible Study is a dynamic, informative, inspiring, and life-changing series that helps you learn about Scripture in a whole new way. Each book will help you explore new dimensions of faith and discover deeper insights for your life as a disciple of Jesus.

The threshold is a place of transition. The threshold of God's word invites you to enter that place where God's truth, goodness, and beauty can shine into your life and fill your mind and heart. Through the Holy Spirit, the threshold becomes holy ground, sacred space, and graced time. God can teach you best at the threshold, because God opens your life to his word and fills you with the Spirit of truth.

With Threshold Bible Study each topic or book of the Bible is approached in a thematic way. You will understand and reflect on the biblical texts through overarching themes derived from biblical theology. Through this method, the study of Scripture will impact your life in a unique way and transform you from within.

These books are designed for maximum flexibility. Each study is presented in a workbook format, with sections for reading, reflecting, writing, discussing, and praying. Each Threshold book contains thirty lessons, which you can use for your daily study over the course of a month or which can be divided into six lessons per week, providing a group study of six weekly sessions. These studies are ideal for Bible study groups, small Christian communities, adult faith formation, student groups, Sunday school, neighborhood groups, and family reading, as well as for individual learning.

The commentary that follows each biblical passage launches your reflection on that passage and helps you begin to see its significance within the context of your contemporary experience. The questions following the commentary challenge you to understand the passage more fully and apply it to your own life. Space for writing after each question is ideal for personal study and also allows group participants to prepare for the weekly discussion. The prayer helps conclude your study each day by integrating your learning into your relationship with God.

The method of Threshold Bible Study is rooted in the ancient tradition of *lectio divina*, whereby studying the Bible becomes a means of deeper intimacy with

God and a transformed life. Reading and interpreting the text (*lectio*) is followed by reflective meditation on its message (*meditatio*). This reading and reflecting flows into prayer from the heart (*oratio* and *contemplatio*). In this way, one listens to God through the Scripture and then responds to God in prayer.

This ancient method assures you that Bible study is a matter of both the mind and the heart. It is not just an intellectual exercise to learn more and be able to discuss the Bible with others. It is, more importantly, a transforming experience. Reflecting on God's word, guided by the Holy Spirit, illumines the mind with wisdom and stirs the heart with zeal.

Following the personal Bible study, Threshold Bible Study offers ways to extend personal *lectio divina* into a weekly conversation with others. This communal experience will allow participants to enhance their appreciation of the message and build up a spiritual community (*collatio*). The end result will be to increase not only individual faith but also faithful witness in the context of daily life (*operatio*).

When bringing Threshold Bible Study to a church community, try to make every effort to include as many people as possible. Many will want to study on their own; others will want to study with family, a group of friends, or a few work associates; some may want to commit themselves to share insights through a weekly conference call, daily text messaging, or an online social network; and others will want to gather weekly in established small groups.

By encouraging Threshold Bible Study and respecting the many ways people desire to make Bible study a regular part of their lives, you will widen the number of people in your church community who study the Bible regularly in whatever way they are able in their busy lives. Simply sign up people at the Sunday services, and order bulk quantities for your church. Encourage people to follow the daily study as faithfully as they can through Sunday announcements, notices in parish publications, support on the church website, and other creative invitations and motivations.

Through the spiritual disciplines of Scripture reading, study, reflection, conversation, and prayer, Threshold Bible Study will help you experience God's grace more abundantly and root your life more deeply in Christ. The risen Jesus said: "Listen! I am standing at the door, knocking; if you hear my voice and open the door, I will come in to you and eat with you, and you with me" (Rev 3:20). Listen to the Word of God, open the door, and cross the threshold to an unimaginable dwelling with God!

SUGGESTIONS FOR INDIVIDUAL STUDY

• Make your Bible reading a time of prayer. Ask for God's guidance as you read the Scriptures.

• Try to study daily, or as often as possible according to the circumstances of your life.

• Read the Bible passage carefully, trying to understand both its meaning and its personal application as you read. Some persons find it helpful to read the passage aloud.

• Read the passage in another Bible translation. Each version adds to your understanding of the original text.

• Allow the commentary to help you comprehend and apply the scriptural text. The commentary is only a beginning, not the last word on the meaning of the passage.

• After reflecting on each question, write out your responses. The very act of writing will help you clarify your thoughts, bring new insights, and amplify your understanding.

• As you reflect on your answers, think about how you can live God's word in the context of your daily life.

• Conclude each daily lesson by reading the prayer and continuing with your own prayer from the heart.

• Make sure your reflections and prayers are matters of both the mind and the heart. A true encounter with God's word is always a transforming experience.

• Choose a word or a phrase from the lesson to carry with you throughout the day as a reminder of your encounter with God's life-changing word.

• Share your learning experience with at least one other person whom you trust for additional insights and affirmation. The ideal way to share learning is in a small group that meets regularly.

SUGGESTIONS FOR GROUP STUDY

• Meet regularly; weekly is ideal. Try to be on time, and make attendance a high priority for the sake of the group. The average group meets for about an hour.

• Open each session with a prepared prayer, a song, or a reflection. Find some appropriate way to bring the group from the workaday world into a sacred time of graced sharing.

• If you have not been together before, name tags are very helpful as group members begin to become acquainted with one another.

• Spend the first session getting acquainted with one another, reading the Introduction aloud and discussing the questions that follow.

• Appoint a group facilitator to provide guidance to the discussion. The role of facilitator may rotate among members each week. The facilitator simply keeps the discussion on track; each person shares responsibility for the group. There is no need for the facilitator to be a trained teacher.

• Try to study the six lessons on your own during the week. When you have done your own reflection and written your own answers, you will be better prepared to discuss the six scriptural lessons with the group. If you have not had an opportunity to study the passages during the week, meet with the group anyway to share support and insights.

• Participate in the discussion as much as you are able, offering your thoughts, insights, feelings, and decisions. You learn by sharing with others the fruits of your study.

• Be careful not to dominate the discussion. It is important that everyone in the group be offered an equal opportunity to share the results of their work. Try to link what you say to the comments of others so that the group remains on the topic.

• When discussing your own personal thoughts or feelings, use "I" language. Be as personal and honest as appropriate, and be very cautious about giving advice to others.

• Listen attentively to the other members of the group so as to learn from their insights. The words of the Bible affect each person in a different way, so a group provides a wealth of understanding for each member.

• Don't fear silence. Silence in a group is as important as silence in personal study. It allows individuals time to listen to the voice of God's Spirit and the opportunity to form their thoughts before they speak.

• Solicit several responses for each question. The thoughts of different people will build on the answers of others and will lead to deeper insights for all.

• Don't fear controversy. Differences of opinions are a sign of a healthy and honest group. If you cannot resolve an issue, continue on, agreeing to disagree. There is probably some truth in each viewpoint.

• Discuss the questions that seem most important for the group. There is no need to cover all the questions in the group session.

• Realize that some questions about the Bible cannot be resolved, even by experts. Don't get stuck on some issue for which there are no clear answers.

• Whatever is said in the group is said in confidence and should be regarded as such.

• Pray as a group in whatever way feels comfortable. Pray for the members of your group throughout the week.

Schedule for Group Study

Session 1: Introduction   Date: _____

Session 2: Lessons 1–6   Date: _____

Session 3: Lessons 7–12   Date: _____

Session 4: Lessons 13–18   Date: _____

Session 5: Lessons 19–24   Date: _____

Session 6: Lessons 25–30   Date: _____

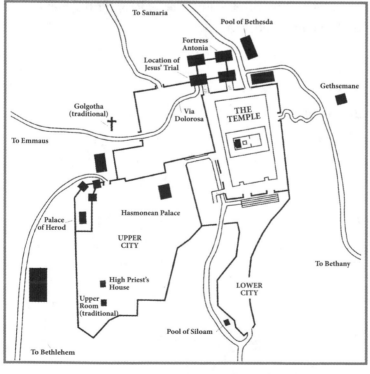

To Samaria

Pool of Bethesda

Fortress
Antonia

Location of
Jesus' Trial

Gethsemane

Golgotha
(traditional)

Via
Dolorosa

THE
TEMPLE

To Emmaus

Hasmonean Palace

Palace
of Herod

UPPER
CITY

To Bethany

High Priest's
House

LOWER
CITY

Upper
Room
(traditional)

Pool of Siloam

To Bethlehem

"The Son of Man came not to be served but to serve, and to give his life a ransom for many." Mark 10:45

Jesus, the Suffering Servant (Part 2)

Mark's gospel is written to help his readers answer two basic questions: Who is Jesus? and What does it mean to be his disciple? The first half of the gospel focused on the question of Jesus' identity, but it left that question open-ended. The second half of the gospel will focus on the question of discipleship, which began in the first half and will intensify as the gospel continues. The two questions are interrelated. An understanding of discipleship requires a clear and correct understanding of Jesus. The more a person is able to understand the meaning of Jesus' life, the more that person is able to understand what it means to follow him as a disciple.

Mark's development of the meaning of discipleship and how best to follow Jesus can be explored on three levels when reading the gospel: first, what Jesus teaches those who follow him about discipleship; second, what Mark teaches his community three or four decades later about discipleship; and, third, what the gospel of Mark teaches us today about discipleship. The experience of following Jesus is not a once-only event for the original disciples. Everyone can come to understand who Jesus is by experiencing him through the inspired word of Mark's gospel and so come to understand what it means to be his disciple. Our response to Jesus is part of the continuing story of the gospel.

1

Mark's interest in discipleship pervades the entire gospel, beginning with the call of Peter, Andrew, James, and John from their fishing careers and ending with the final invitation to the disciples and Peter at the empty tomb. The term "disciples" is used over forty times in Mark's gospel, and "the Twelve" another ten times. For Mark, the disciples represent the church to which he addresses his gospel, the Christian community in Rome, and later believers in each generation. The Twelve represent church leaders, in Mark's community and in every age.

Discipleship that developed during the ministry of Jesus, discipleship in the early church of Rome, and discipleship throughout the centuries are joined together through the resurrection of Jesus. For the gospel of Mark, the resurrection is not so much the end of the gospel but, rather, the beginning. The life of Jesus is good news because he is risen. It is the reason that discipleship can be lived over and over again in the lives of each generation of Christians.

And so we join with disciples in every age to follow Jesus. As we enter the narrative of Mark's gospel, we learn from Jesus and his original disciples how to be a follower of the Risen Jesus today. Through the process of listening, reflecting, and praying, these texts of the gospel become our own and we find our place within the community of disciples.

Reflection and discussion

• What is the relationship between the two basic questions of Mark's gospel?

• How does Mark's gospel link the original disciples of Jesus with disciples in the church today?

Learning though the Successes and Failures of the Original Disciples

The gospel of Mark teaches about true discipleship by using two approaches: the via positiva and the via negativa. The disciples of Jesus are portrayed positively, so that readers can identify with them and become like them. Even more significantly, the disciples are portrayed negatively, enabling readers to see their misunderstandings and mistakes, even their denial and betrayal, to learn from their failures.

We see the disciples in a positive light at their call. Peter, Andrew, James, and John respond generously, leaving all to follow Jesus. They put their fate and their future into the hands of the master. They commit themselves to an unknown and uncertain future and to a totally new way of life. We see the Twelve as the intimate companions of Jesus as he teaches them about the mystery of the kingdom of God and as he explains to them his parables and sayings. Then, after being with Jesus, they are sent out by him on mission—to preach, drive out demons, and heal. The disciples continue following Jesus along his way, accompanying him on his fateful journey to Jerusalem.

We also see the disciples in a negative light through their failures. Throughout the first half of the Gospel, the disciples are continually unable to understand Jesus and what he has done. Over and over Jesus asks them: "Do you not yet understand or comprehend? Are your hearts hardened? Do you have eyes and not see, ears and not hear?" When Jesus heals the deaf man and then heals the blind man, surely Jesus is also seeking to heal the deafness and the blindness of all his followers.

In the second half of the gospel, as Jesus begins to teach his disciples that he must suffer, die, and rise, he also teaches them about discipleship. Each time Jesus predicts his own passion, it is met by misunderstanding and resistance on the part of his disciples. Jesus responds each time by teaching them the intimate connection between who he is and what it means to be his disciple. This pattern is repeated three times as Jesus travels with his disciples from Galilee toward Jerusalem.

Following the first passion prediction of Jesus (8:31), Peter rebukes Jesus because he cannot accept the idea of a suffering Messiah (8:32–33). Jesus then teaches that whoever chooses to be disciples must deny themselves, take up the cross, and follow (8:34–35). Following Jesus' second prediction of the passion, the disciples argue over who is the greatest (9:32–34). Jesus then teaches them that a disciple is to be the last of all and the servant of all (9:35–37). Following Jesus' third and final prediction of the passion, James and John request places of honor when Jesus enters his glory (10:35–37). In teaching his disciples, Jesus rejects the way that power was exercised in the Roman world of his day. He dramatically reverses the standards of the world and shows that Isaiah's Suffering Servant—the one who gives his life for others—is the model both for his life and that of his disciples.

This section of the gospel is framed by two accounts of people restored to sight by Jesus: the blind man at Bethsaida, who gradually comes to see clearly, and the blind Bartimaeus, who, after receiving his sight, follows Jesus along the way. Jesus, in this section, is trying to heal the spiritual blindness of his disciples. By his teaching, he tries to open their eyes to new dimensions of discipleship. Jesus wants them to see that he is to suffer and die, and to see the significance of this for their discipleship. Like the gradual healing of the blind man at Bethsaida, the disciples gradually come to understand Jesus and their own discipleship. This step-by-step teaching of Jesus on discipleship occurs as Jesus and his followers travel toward the cross in Jerusalem.

The misunderstanding of the disciples in each of these three cycles of teaching points out three dangerous tendencies in Christian discipleship for every age: denial of suffering, desire for personal prestige, and competitiveness. The education Jesus gives them on the nature of true discipleship includes instructions intended for every age of the church. They are a summary of Jesus' primary teachings on the nature of discipleship and the qualities necessary for one who claims to be his follower.

Reflection and discussion

• What have I learned in the first half of Mark's gospel from the example of the disciples?

• Why would Mark so insistently emphasize the failures of Jesus' disciples?

Following Jesus to the Cross

In the passion account, the failures of the disciples are seen most dramatically. The confident Peter denies Jesus three times. His closest followers fall asleep in the garden. Judas betrays Jesus with a kiss. All his disciples leave him and flee at his darkest hour. No disciple stands at the foot of the cross in Mark's gospel. Every one of them has good intentions and a real desire to follow Jesus to the end. Yet, they do not understand Jesus' continual teaching about the necessity of the cross.

Ironically, it is the minor characters of the gospel who respond best to the demands of discipleship. The blind man Bartimaeus follows Jesus to Jerusalem. The woman at Bethany anoints Jesus despite the protests of his disciples. The Gentile centurion at the cross proclaims the faith that the disciples of Jesus should have understood. The women who followed Jesus from Galilee continue to minister to him in life and in death. A member of the Jewish council, Joseph of Arimathea, is the only one courageous enough to approach Pilate and give Jesus a proper burial.

Readers of Mark's gospel in every age readily identify with the disciples. They reflect the enthusiasms, misunderstandings, and failures characteristic of the church in Mark's community and of the church in every succeeding generation. As the grumbling of Israel in the desert was written down for the instruction of each succeeding generation, so the misunderstandings and failures of the disciples of Jesus are written down for our instruction. When Jesus calls his disciples to follow him, he is calling us. When Jesus rebukes his disciples for their failure to understand, we stand convicted. When the disciples betray, deny, and abandon Jesus, we know that we have done the same. Yet, we are also confronted with the forgiveness of Jesus and offered the hope of another chance to follow him.

The fact that Mark's gospel is open-ended offers readers in every age the opportunity to identify with those first disciples. The good news of Mark is that, despite our failures, Jesus has authority on earth to forgive sins and constantly renews the call to follow him. Through the disciples of Jesus in the gospel, Mark illustrates the true meaning of discipleship for all times. Mark demonstrates for his own community and for ours that the disciple is not one who sits back and reaps the benefits of being a Christian. The cross of Jesus, the Suffering Servant, presents a challenge for all who choose to be followers of the Risen Lord.

Reflection and discussion

• How could the disciples continually fail to understand Jesus, even all the way to the cross?

• What do I hope to learn about following Jesus during the second half of Mark's gospel?

The End is the New Beginning

The other three gospel accounts in the New Testament begin much more elaborately and end much more gloriously than the account of Mark. The gospels of Matthew and Luke begin with detailed infancy narratives of Jesus, and John's gospel begins with his dramatic prologue on the Word of God. Each of these three gospels ends with remarkable appearances of the risen

Jesus. Mark's gospel has none of this. The gospel begins with a one-verse intro announcing "the good news of Jesus Christ, the Son of God." It concludes abruptly with the empty tomb of Jesus, a promise that Jesus will see his disciples in Galilee, and the fear and flight of the women (16:6–8). As we will see, the other endings of Mark are clearly added later by another author in imitation of the other gospels. There are no resurrection appearances in Mark's gospel. Rather, it concludes with hopeful uncertainty.

Yet, despite the failure of the disciples and the fearful flight of the women, the promise given at the end of the gospel surely was fulfilled. The risen Jesus did indeed encounter his disciples in Galilee, and the church arose from that meeting. For that reason, the gospel of Mark proclaims a confident hope for failed, frightened, and fleeing disciples in every generation.

The gospel was written in and for the church, the ongoing community of disciples. The Roman setting in which Mark wrote his gospel has many parallels to the situation of believers in the church today. Rome was a culture desperately in need of the gospel, but which fought it mightily. In many parts of the world today, professing Christian faith puts one at risk of persecution, discrimination, and suffering. Even in places with a history of Christian culture, commitment to Jesus Christ can bring alienation from family, colleagues, and associations. Seeking to evangelize the culture today often leads to condescension, exclusion, and hostility. In this context, Mark's gospel offers insights, challenges, and encouragement for the church of our time.

Because Jesus is risen, all that he said and did during his earthly life are not merely events of history but present and future sources of evangelical power. A reflective and prayerful reading of the gospel brings us into living contact with Jesus through the working of the Holy Spirit. When we experience flaws and failure in discipleship, Jesus promises to manifest himself with his forgiveness and grace.

Reflection and discussion

• In what ways does a reflective and prayerful reading of the gospel offer me hope?

• How does the resurrection of Jesus and the power of the Holy Spirit influence the way that I read the gospel?

Prayer

Father of Jesus, your only Son healed the deaf and the blind, but his disciples failed to hear his teachings and closed their eyes to his saving deeds. As I continue to study this gospel of Mark, guide me to faith and hope in Jesus. As I follow Jesus from Galilee to the cross, form me as an obedient disciple, trusting in your grace. Let your Spirit come upon me to guide my reflection and prayer so that I may remain faithful to the challenge of living the good news according to Mark.

SUGGESTIONS FOR FACILITATORS, GROUP SESSION 1

1. If the group is meeting for the first time, or if there are newcomers joining the group, it is helpful to provide nametags.

2. Distribute the books to the members of the group.

3. You may want to ask the participants to introduce themselves and tell the group a bit about themselves.

4. Ask one or more of these introductory questions:
   • What drew you to join this group?
   • What is your biggest fear in beginning this Bible study?
   • How is beginning this study like a "threshold" for you?

5. You may want to pray this prayer as a group:

Come upon us, Holy Spirit, to enlighten and guide us as we continue this study of Mark's gospel. You inspired the biblical writers to reveal your presence throughout the history of salvation. This inspired word has the power to convert our hearts and change our lives. Fill our hearts with desire, trust, and confidence as you shine the light of your truth within us. Motivate us to read the Scriptures, and give us a deeper love for God's word each day. Bless us during this session and throughout the coming week with the fire of your love.

6. Read the Introduction aloud, pausing at each question for discussion. Group members may wish to write the insights of the group as each question is discussed. Encourage several members of the group to respond to each question.

7. Don't feel compelled to finish the complete Introduction during the session. It is better to allow sufficient time to talk about the questions raised than to rush to the end. Group members may read any remaining sections on their own after the group meeting.

8. Instruct group members to read the first six lessons on their own during the six days before the next group meeting. They should write out their own answers to the questions as preparation for next week's group discussion.

9. Fill in the date for each group meeting under "Schedule for Group Study."

10. Conclude by praying aloud together the prayer at the end of the Introduction.

**Then Jesus laid his hands on his eyes again;
and he looked intently and his sight was restored,
and he saw everything clearly.**

Mark 8:25

Gradually Coming to See and Understand Jesus

MARK 8:22–30 *²²They came to Bethsaida. Some people brought a blind man to him and begged him to touch him. ²³He took the blind man by the hand and led him out of the village; and when he had put saliva on his eyes and laid his hands on him, he asked him, "Can you see anything?" ²⁴And the man looked up and said, "I can see people, but they look like trees, walking." ²⁵Then Jesus laid his hands on his eyes again; and he looked intently and his sight was restored, and he saw everything clearly. ²⁶Then he sent him away to his home, saying, "Do not even go into the village." ²⁷Jesus went on with his disciples to the villages of Caesarea Philippi; and on the way he asked his disciples, "Who do people say that I am?" ²⁸And they answered him, "John the Baptist; and others, Elijah; and still others, one of the prophets." ²⁹He asked them, "But who do you say that I am?" Peter answered him, "You are the Messiah." ³⁰And he sternly ordered them not to tell anyone about him.*

T he healing of the blind man serves as a hinge connecting the first and second half of Mark's gospel. It culminates all the previous healing accounts demonstrating Jesus' messianic power. It is particularly linked to the previous healing of the deaf man with the speech impediment. These two healing accounts are similar in several ways. In both accounts, Jesus takes the afflicted person away from the crowd, indicating the separation from one's past that Jesus' message demands (verse 23). In both accounts, Jesus uses bodily signs, including spittle and touch, as instruments of healing. With these two miracles, Jesus completes the prophecy of Isaiah describing the works of the coming Messiah: "Then the eyes of the blind shall be opened, and the ears of the deaf unstopped; then the lame shall leap like a deer, and the tongue of the speechless sing for joy" (Isa 35:5–6).

The healing of the blind man also begins the second half of the gospel which will emphasize the failure of the disciples to understand the full significance of Jesus' messianic identity. The miracle is unique in that it occurs in two stages. At the first stage of healing, the man seems to be severely near-sighted, with things at a distance appearing quite blurry (verse 24). But Jesus will not leave the man with only partial sight. Finally, following a second touch of Jesus, the man is fully healed and able to see everything clearly (verse 25). The account provides the introduction to the rest of the gospel which will emphasize the limited insight of the disciples and their need for a more complete perception of the meaning of Jesus' mission.

Immediately following the healing of the blind man, Jesus travels with the disciples "on the way" (verse 27). In this travel narrative, which will end in Jerusalem, Jesus will teach his followers "the way" of true discipleship. So, first he asks them, "Who do people say that I am?" Their response is similar to the list given earlier when Herod heard about Jesus. He might be John the Baptist, Elijah, or another of the prophets. Then, Jesus asks his disciples directly, "But who do you say that I am?" (verse 29). This is the central question of the gospel. The question of Jesus' true identity leaps off the pages of history and into the heart of every reader of the gospel. The first half of the gospel has led up to this question. Jesus has revealed himself as a teacher and healer with divine authority, the bridegroom, the Lord of the Sabbath, the sower of God's word, the great physician, and the shepherd who feeds God's people. Yet, he has also met with persistent resistance and continual misunderstanding. His teaching in parables and his great deeds have both revealed and concealed his true identity. "Who do you say I am?" must be answered completely by every individual who chooses to be his disciple.

Peter answers for the disciples, "You are the Messiah." His insightful response represents a dramatic breakthrough in the gospel. He recognizes Jesus as the one through whom God will accomplish all that he promised. Yet, while Peter's identification of Jesus is correct, the gospel will soon demonstrate that Peter and the others still have a totally inaccurate understanding of what Jesus' identity as the Messiah entails.

The journey of Jesus with his disciples to Jerusalem will conclude with a second healing of a blind man. These two accounts form a frame around the journey narrative and symbolize the disciples' gradual growth in understanding. With their eyes now partly open to understand Jesus as the Messiah, their understanding is still distorted and nearsighted. They will need further enlightenment to understand that Jesus is also the Suffering Servant whose full identity can only be revealed at the cross.

Reflection and discussion

• In what ways does the healing of the blind man connect the first and second halves of the gospel?

• How does the healing of the blind man form a metaphor for the understanding of Jesus' disciples?

• In what way does the nearsightedness of the partially healed blind man express the understanding of the disciples?

• What are some of the mistaken understandings of Jesus that people hold today?

• How has my reflecting on this gospel helped me to understand Jesus more fully? How do I answer the question of Jesus, "Who do you say I am?"

Prayer

Jesus, heal the blindness that prevents me from knowing you and seeing your will for me. Guide me as I journey with you and your disciples along the way to Jerusalem. Deepen my understanding of you as I approach your cross.

"For those who want to save their life will lose it,
and those who lose their life for my sake, and for the
sake of the gospel, will save it." Mark 8:35

Instructions on Discipleship

MARK 8:31–9:1 *³¹Then he began to teach them that the Son of Man must undergo great suffering, and be rejected by the elders, the chief priests, and the scribes, and be killed, and after three days rise again. ³²He said all this quite openly. And Peter took him aside and began to rebuke him. ³³But turning and looking at his disciples, he rebuked Peter and said, "Get behind me, Satan! For you are setting your mind not on divine things but on human things."*

³⁴He called the crowd with his disciples, and said to them, "If any want to become my followers, let them deny themselves and take up their cross and follow me. ³⁵ For those who want to save their life will lose it, and those who lose their life for my sake, and for the sake of the gospel, will save it. ³⁶For what will it profit them to gain the whole world and forfeit their life? ³⁷Indeed, what can they give in return for their life? ³⁸Those who are ashamed of me and of my words in this adulterous and sinful generation, of them the Son of Man will also be ashamed when he comes in the glory of his Father with the holy angels."

9 ¹And he said to them, "Truly I tell you, there are some standing here who will not taste death until they see that the kingdom of God has come with power."

The notice that Jesus "began to teach them" marks a new stage in Jesus' ministry and a sharp change of tone. Leaving behind his method of teaching the mystery in parables to the crowd, he now instructs his disciples on the necessity of his suffering, rejection, and death. This first prediction of his passion is Jesus' direct response to Peter's proclamation that Jesus is the Messiah. If the disciples have begun to realize his messianic identity, then Jesus can begin to reveal what that implies for his destiny. In each of his three passion predictions, Jesus will refer to himself as the Son of Man, his favorite self-designation and a title that paradoxically includes both his humility and his glory. Jesus' insistence that the Son of Man "must" undergo his passion and death, then rise three days later, implies that this horrible defeat and glorious victory are not a historical mistake or accident, but in fact the plan of God.

The shock caused by Jesus' words leads Peter to rebuke Jesus (verse 32). Though Peter is correct in understanding that Jesus is the Messiah, he refuses to accept Jesus' interpretation of his messianic role. Peter and most Jews of the time thought that Israel's Messiah would be a conqueror. Peter rejects any association of Jesus with failure, suffering, and death. Yet, after Peter rebukes his Master, Jesus rebukes Peter in the strongest words of the gospel: "Get behind me, Satan!" Jesus is not suggesting that Peter is possessed by the devil, but that Peter is acting like Satan by tempting Jesus to deny his true mission and God's saving plan. Playing the role of the satanic adversary, Peter is trying to draw Jesus in the direction of triumphal success and to dissuade Jesus from the cross.

Jesus' response to Peter is a warning for anyone in any age who refuses to place a supreme value on the sacrificial death of Jesus. Jesus rebukes Peter's false triumphalism, just as he rejects worldly success in religious practice today. Jesus accuses Peter of setting his mind "not on divine things but on human things." It is thoroughly human to avoid humiliation, suffering, and failure, and Peter's response is totally in line with the values of the world. Yet, Jesus calls his followers to the divine plan, in which Jesus would give his life for the salvation of the world. Human ways are no longer enough, because according to human reasoning the cross makes no sense. Instead, Jesus calls his disciples to a divine way of thinking that involves a conversion of heart.

Jesus begins to describe this conversion of heart that is required for discipleship. He teaches that those wishing to be his disciples must do three things:

deny themselves, take up their cross, and follow him (verse 34). Self-denial is not just a type of discipline or ascetic practice; rather, it means denying that the self is the one who determines the aspirations and goals of one's life. Taking up the cross means that the disciple must be willing to shoulder humiliation, suffering, and even torturous death if necessary, in order to follow Jesus. Disciples must be in constant contact with Jesus, letting him go ahead of them, and continually following his lead every step of the way.

Jesus then provides reasons for accepting the invitation to discipleship. Those who wish to save their lives for their own sake will lose their lives. But those who lose their lives for the sake of Jesus and the gospel will achieve eternal salvation (verse 35). This paradoxical teaching means that those who deny themselves, take up the cross, and follow Jesus will obtain life in its fullness. Any material gains in power, wealth, or pleasure are useless for those who have forfeited their very selves in the process (verse 36).

Jesus refers for the first time to his final coming, when the Son of Man "comes in the glory of his Father with the holy angels" (verse 38). On that day, our relationship to Jesus will determine our eternal destiny. Those who have identified their lives with his by sharing in his cross will remain united with him in resurrection. Jesus assures his audience that some of them will see the coming of God's kingdom with power before their death (9:1). The meaning of Jesus' promise will be clearer as Jesus approaches the cross with his disciples.

Reflection and discussion

• Why did Peter rebuke Jesus? Why did Jesus rebuke Peter?

• How does Peter show himself to be like the partially healed blind man of the previous narrative?

• How would I explain the teaching of Jesus in verse 35 to another person?

• What are the implications of following a Messiah who promises us a share in his suffering? What are some ways in which I may be called to deny myself for the sake of Jesus and the gospel?

Prayer

Suffering Lord, I want to know you more fully and to follow you wherever you lead. Give me the courage to be your disciple by denying myself, taking up the cross, and following wherever you lead me.

Then Peter said to Jesus, "Rabbi, it is good for us
to be here; let us make three dwellings, one for you,
one for Moses, and one for Elijah."

Mark 9:5

Mountaintop Glory
with Moses and Elijah

MARK 9:2–13 ²*Six days later, Jesus took with him Peter and James and John, and led them up a high mountain apart, by themselves. And he was transfigured before them, ³and his clothes became dazzling white, such as no one on earth could bleach them. ⁴And there appeared to them Elijah with Moses, who were talking with Jesus. ⁵Then Peter said to Jesus, "Rabbi, it is good for us to be here; let us make three dwellings, one for you, one for Moses, and one for Elijah." ⁶He did not know what to say, for they were terrified. ⁷Then a cloud overshadowed them, and from the cloud there came a voice, "This is my Son, the Beloved; listen to him!" ⁸Suddenly when they looked around, they saw no one with them any more, but only Jesus.*

⁹*As they were coming down the mountain, he ordered them to tell no one about what they had seen, until after the Son of Man had risen from the dead. ¹⁰So they kept the matter to themselves, questioning what this rising from the dead could mean. ¹¹Then they asked him, "Why do the scribes say that Elijah must come first?" ¹²He said to them, "Elijah is indeed coming first to restore all things. How then is it written about the Son of Man, that he is to go through*

many sufferings and be treated with contempt? ¹³*But I tell you that Elijah has come, and they did to him whatever they pleased, as it is written about him."*

The reader of the gospel is aware of Jesus' relationship to God from the opening verse proclaiming Jesus as God's Son and from the revelation given to Jesus at his baptism. But here, the revelation is given to Peter, James, and John in dramatic fashion on the mountain. As Moses went up Mount Sinai to encounter God and Elijah went to that same mountain to hear God's whispering yet transforming voice, Jesus ascends a high mountain with his closest disciples for a divine manifestation. He offers them a fleeting glimpse and encouraging insight into the fullness of the divine mystery veiled by his humanity.

This transfiguration of Jesus occurs immediately after Jesus began to teach his disciples about the cost of discipleship. As Jesus leads them to the cross, he presents Elijah and Moses to them and offers a foretaste of his glory which he will enter through his death and resurrection. Elijah and Moses anticipated the way of the cross through their difficult lives of hearing and obeying God's will. These two central figures of the Old Testament prepared the way of Jesus in the long drama of the world's salvation. The revelation of the glorified Jesus with Moses and Elijah also anticipates the glory that Peter, James, and John will experience if they walk the way of his cross.

Peter's instincts are correct in suggesting that he erect three "dwellings" on the spot (verse 4). The word indicates the temporary, makeshift shelters erected during the Jewish Feast of Sukkoth to remember Israel's forty-year journey through the desert. Peter's remembrance of the saving path of Exodus is a reminder that the disciples are still on the way with Jesus. As Elijah and Moses prepared his way, Jesus prepares Peter, James, and John to travel with him to Jerusalem and to continue his way into the early church. Uncertain of where their journey will lead, these disciples will be models of Christian discipleship for future generations.

From the overshadowing cloud, God reveals the identity of Jesus to Peter, James, and John: "This is my Son, the Beloved" (verse 7). God's voice then commands the disciples, "Listen to him!" Listening to Jesus means both hearing and obeying what he says. As the disciples continue the journey with Jesus to Jerusalem, they must keep listening to what Jesus teaches them and live by those teachings. Listening to Jesus is the way to follow in his way—listening to the word of God that transfigures sinners into forgiven and redeemed people, that transfigures sick and disabled bodies into healed and whole beings, that transfigures bread and wine into his body and blood, that transfigures suffering and death into resurrected life.

As they were coming down the mountain, Jesus orders his three disciples to tell no one what they had seen until after his resurrection. People would easily accept a glorious Messiah, but the glory of Jesus cannot be understood apart from his death and resurrection. Jesus continues to use the title Son of Man for himself because his divine sonship cannot be comprehended yet. The disciples cannot yet accept a Messiah who must suffer and die on the way to glory, so they continue to question what "rising from the dead" could mean (verse 10).

The disciples continue questioning how God's kingdom has come according to the teachings of the ancient Scriptures (verses 11–13). First, they ask about the coming of Elijah, whom the Scriptures foretold would come to prepare the way (Mal 4:5). In response Jesus affirms that Elijah has already come in the person of John the Baptist. Second, they ask why the Messiah must go through many sufferings and be treated with contempt. Although Jesus does not respond here, he will continue to teach how he is the Suffering Servant, the one whom Isaiah said would suffer greatly and be rejected, pouring out himself to death and bearing the sins of many (Isa 53).

Reflection and discussion

• In what ways does the transfiguration show how Elijah and Moses prepared God's people for the way of Jesus?

• Why did Jesus bring Peter, James, and John by themselves to the high mountain? Why did God reveal the most important figures of the Old Testament to the most important figures of the early church?

• How might Peter have felt during this experience? Why did he want to make three dwellings?

• God tells the disciples to "listen" to Jesus as he teaches them along the journey toward Jerusalem. As I listen to Jesus through this gospel, what am I being challenged to believe or to do?

Prayer

Transfigured Lord, though I want to stay with you on the mountain, you call me to descend with you to life's valleys. Teach me to listen to you so that I may obey and follow in the way you desire for my life.

Immediately the father of the child cried out,
"I believe; help my unbelief!" Mark 9:24

The Boy Possessed
by an Unclean Spirit

MARK 9:14–29 ¹⁴*When they came to the disciples, they saw a great crowd around them, and some scribes arguing with them.* ¹⁵*When the whole crowd saw him, they were immediately overcome with awe, and they ran forward to greet him.* ¹⁶*He asked them, "What are you arguing about with them?"* ¹⁷*Someone from the crowd answered him, "Teacher, I brought you my son; he has a spirit that makes him unable to speak;* ¹⁸*and whenever it seizes him, it dashes him down; and he foams and grinds his teeth and becomes rigid; and I asked your disciples to cast it out, but they could not do so."* ¹⁹*He answered them, "You faithless generation, how much longer must I be among you? How much longer must I put up with you? Bring him to me."* ²⁰*And they brought the boy to him. When the spirit saw him, immediately it convulsed the boy, and he fell on the ground and rolled about, foaming at the mouth.* ²¹*Jesus asked the father, "How long has this been happening to him?" And he said, "From childhood.* ²²*It has often cast him into the fire and into the water, to destroy him; but if you are able to do anything, have pity on us and help us."* ²³*Jesus said to him, "If you are able!—All things can be done for the one who believes."* ²⁴*Immediately the father of the child cried out, "I believe; help my unbelief!"* ²⁵*When Jesus saw that a crowd came running together, he rebuked the unclean spirit, saying to it, "You spirit that* *keeps this boy from speaking and hearing, I command you, come out of him, and never enter him again!" ²⁶After crying out and convulsing him terribly, it came out, and the boy was like a corpse, so that most of them said, "He is dead." ²⁷But Jesus took him by the hand and lifted him up, and he was able to stand. ²⁸When he had entered the house, his disciples asked him privately, "Why could we not cast it out?" ²⁹He said to them, "This kind can come out only through prayer."*

Jesus and the three disciples return from the mountain of Jesus' glorious transfiguration to a scene of confusion. The scribes have entered into another argument with the crowd, the man who had brought his son to be healed is ready to give up, and the disciples were frustrated at their inability to expel the evil spirit from the boy. Clearly the experience of glory is only momentary in the life of discipleship. The scene is reminiscent of the return of Moses from his mountaintop encounter to find faithlessness on the part of Israel (Exod 32). Jesus' frustrated response to the situation, "You faithless generation, how much longer must I be among you?" expresses dissatisfaction that his disciples were not yet able to minister with faith and power in his absence. Away from the mountaintop, unbelief is a constant risk, and the power of evil must always be confronted. Jesus must continue to teach his disciples what it means to follow in the way of the suffering Messiah.

Just as Jesus was revealed at his baptism as God's beloved Son and then confronted Satan in the wilderness, the revelation of Jesus at the transfiguration is followed by this conflict with an evil spirit. The father of the boy explains that he brought his son to Jesus, but discovering that Jesus was away, he asked the disciples to cast out the spirit. Since Jesus had given the Twelve authority over unclean spirits, and with that authority they had cast out many demons and healed many who were sick (6:7, 13), the man assumed that the remaining nine would be able to do what Jesus could do.

The inability to expel the demon is described as a lack of belief and prayer on the part of both the father and the disciples. Repeating the words of the father, "If you are able!" Jesus assures both the father and his disciples that "all things can be done for the one who believes" (verse 23). Lack of faith hinders the work of God. Jesus' power to overcome evil is not at issue; rather, the need for trust in that power by the father and the disciples is the key to this narrative. The blindness, unbelief, and failure of the disciples to understand have brought them to this point where they are unable to cast out a demon and heal the boy. The father, on the other hand, admits his struggle to believe and cries out for the gift of faith: "I believe; help my unbelief!" (verse 24). His statement is one of the most beloved verses in Scripture because it expresses the mixed character of faith within the experience of most people.

The father's heartfelt cry, his desire to overcome his doubts, and his quest for a deeper faith open the door for Jesus' power to overcome evil in his son. Jesus commands the demon not only to come out of the boy, but to never enter him again. The spirit's hold on the boy is broken and it leaves him with a final convulsion. The departing attack is so violent that the boy became like a corpse (verse 26). Jesus' lifting him up so that he is able to stand recalls the earlier raisings of Peter's mother-in-law from sickness and Jairus' daughter from death. The language is that of resurrection, foreshadowing both the resurrection of Jesus and his promise to raise his followers from death.

The private words of Jesus to his disciples when they are back in the house teach them why they were unable to free the boy from the evil spirit. He tells them to rely on prayer, which expresses dependence on God and trust in him. His words suggest that the disciples have begun to neglect their need to depend completely on God. The spiritual gifts of healing or exorcisms are not personal achievements, but are demonstrations of God working through human ministers. Their future ministry in the church will bear fruit only as they humble themselves and bring their needs to Jesus in prayer.

Reflection and discussion

• What are some of the reasons the disciples were not able to free the boy from the evil spirit apart from the presence of Jesus?

• How is this account about the need to trust Jesus on the part of the father and the disciples? What does it mean to say, "All things can be done for the one who believes"?

• Why did the cry of the father, "I believe; help my unbelief," open the door for Jesus' power? Why do his words resonate so clearly with all who struggle with faith?

• What connections do I find between my faith, my ministry, and my prayer?

Prayer

Divine Teacher, I believe; help my unbelief. Show me what it means to have faith in you and to trust in your presence. Continue to teach me and keep me close to you in prayer, so that I may be your trustworthy disciple.

Jesus sat down, called the twelve, and said to them, "Whoever wants to be first must be last of all and servant of all." Mark 9:35

More Instructions for Failing Disciples

MARK 9:30–37 ³⁰*They went on from there and passed through Galilee. He did not want anyone to know it;* ³¹*for he was teaching his disciples, saying to them, "The Son of Man is to be betrayed into human hands, and they will kill him, and three days after being killed, he will rise again."* ³²*But they did not understand what he was saying and were afraid to ask him.*

³³*Then they came to Capernaum; and when he was in the house he asked them, "What were you arguing about on the way?"* ³⁴*But they were silent, for on the way they had argued with one another who was the greatest.* ³⁵*He sat down, called the twelve, and said to them, "Whoever wants to be first must be last of all and servant of all."* ³⁶*Then he took a little child and put it among them; and taking it in his arms, he said to them,* ³⁷*"Whoever welcomes one such child in my name welcomes me, and whoever welcomes me welcomes not me but the one who sent me."*

As Jesus continues "on the way," traveling with his disciples through Galilee and toward Jerusalem, he offers his second announcement of his passion. Jesus does not want anyone to know his whereabouts because he is instructing his disciples privately and wants to have their full attention. As with his first prediction, Jesus' words are followed by indications that his disciples fail to grasp the most essential elements of being his follower. According to the previous pattern, their misunderstanding and resistance become the occasion for another teaching of Jesus on the intimate connection between who he is and what it means to be his disciple.

As in his first announcement of the passion, Jesus refers to himself as the Son of Man and predicts that he will be killed, but also that he will rise from death three days later (verse 31). In addition, Jesus states that he will be "betrayed into human hands," emphasizing the culpability of all humanity, rather than simply the religious leaders. Again, the disciples fail to understand the divine necessity and the implications of what Jesus is saying. Not only is Jesus teaching his disciples about the significance of his approaching passion, but Mark is teaching his readers that the death of Jesus is not an unfortunate tragedy. Rather, it is the heart of the divine plan for humanity's salvation. As the suffering Messiah, Jesus is determined to carry out the Father's will, despite the fear and confusion of his followers.

The disciples' failure to understand that the way of the Messiah is the way of the cross becomes painfully obvious as they argue with one another over who is the greatest (verse 34). Clearly they did not comprehend the implications of Jesus' passion on their own leadership roles within the emerging church. Their competition for top honors is the exact opposite of what they should have been seeking as followers of Jesus. They must begin to judge and act according to the values of God's reign rather than the values of the world. For Jesus, humble service of others is the mark of true greatness and genuine discipleship.

Jesus uses his disciples' mistake as the opportunity for teaching. Calling the Twelve, those specially singled for roles of leadership among Jesus' followers, he says to them, "Whoever wants to be first must be last of all and servant of all" (verse 35). In the world of ancient Rome, where humility and meekness were considered signs of weakness, this was a radically unconventional idea. Rulers, aristocrats, and those with authority expected to be served and showered with honors. But Jesus turns the established order upside down. The "first" or the greatest in the reign of God is the person at the end or at the bottom. Genuine leaders in the way of Jesus are the servants of all those they lead.

Jesus follows his teaching with a symbolic action to reinforce his message. He places a little child in the midst of the Twelve. Then, while holding the child in his arms, he says, "Whoever welcomes one such child in my name welcomes me." In the society of Jesus' day, children were inconsequential and totally dependent on others; they had no legal rights or status. So, Jesus is teaching the future leaders of his church to esteem and serve those who are the most helpless and cannot repay their service. Jesus himself identifies with those who are most insignificant in the eyes of human society, so that when his disciples welcome the poor, the outcasts, the nobodies, and the neediest, they are truly welcoming him. Moreover, Jesus says, "Whoever welcomes me welcomes not me but the one who sent me." Since Jesus has been sent from the Father, then those who serve Jesus through serving the insignificant are actually serving God.

Reflection and discussion

• What are the differences between the idea of success that is promoted in today's marketplace and the idea of success endorsed by Jesus?

• What is the impression Jesus wished to leave on the future leaders of his church by placing the child in their midst?

Prayer

Suffering Messiah, you taught your chosen Twelve to be the last of all and the servants of all. Help me to see your image in those who are most lowly and helpless. Help me to accept, serve, and care for those who are least important in the world.

"Truly I tell you, whoever gives you a
cup of water to drink because you bear the
name of Christ will by no means lose the reward."

Mark 9:41

Advice and Warning for Disciples

MARK 9:38–50 *[38]John said to him, "Teacher, we saw someone casting out demons in your name, and we tried to stop him, because he was not following us." [39]But Jesus said, "Do not stop him; for no one who does a deed of power in my name will be able soon afterward to speak evil of me. [40]Whoever is not against us is for us. [41]For truly I tell you, whoever gives you a cup of water to drink because you bear the name of Christ will by no means lose the reward.*

[42]"If any of you put a stumbling block before one of these little ones who believe in me, it would be better for you if a great millstone were hung around your neck and you were thrown into the sea. [43]If your hand causes you to stumble, cut it off; it is better for you to enter life maimed than to have two hands and to go to hell, to the unquenchable fire. [45]And if your foot causes you to stumble, cut it off; it is better for you to enter life lame than to have two feet and to be thrown into hell. [47]And if your eye causes you to stumble, tear it out; it is better for you to enter the kingdom of God with one eye than to have two eyes and to be thrown into hell, [48]where their worm never dies, and the fire is never quenched.

⁴⁹*"For everyone will be salted with fire. ⁵⁰Salt is good; but if salt has lost its saltiness, how can you season it? Have salt in yourselves, and be at peace with one another."*

As Jesus continues to teach his close disciples about the kind of service they must offer to others, John speaks up to inform Jesus about someone who was expelling demons in the name of Jesus, but who carried out his ministry outside the circle of the Twelve. John says, "We tried to stop him because he was not following us." The disciples' opposition to the successful exorcist is striking especially in light of their recent failure to cast out an evil spirit (9:18). Jesus reproves his disciples: "Do not stop him." Anyone who does a deed of power in Jesus' name is not an adversary, but rather gives honor to Jesus.

The account echoes the incident in the book of Numbers when Joshua noticed that two men were employing the gift of prophecy though they had not been among the seventy elders officially commissioned with the spirit of Moses. Joshua said, "My lord Moses, stop them!" But Moses replied, "Are you jealous for my sake? Would that all the Lord's people were prophets, and that the Lord would put his spirit on them!" (Num 11:24–30). Like Moses before him, Jesus directs his disciples to have an open mind and heart toward those who are not within the formal bounds of the community.

Even those who do the smallest and simplest acts of service, like giving a cup of water in the name of Christ, will be rewarded by God (verse 41). All of these unnamed servants are following in the way of Jesus, even though they might not be formally designated as inside the band of Jesus and his church. God's love is inclusive, and Jesus will give up his life for all. Jesus will leave behind an open way to God for all. There is no place for exclusivism and intolerance among those who follow Jesus as his disciples.

After Jesus teaches his disciples about the gracious rewards in store for those who demonstrate humble service, he warns them about the terrible consequences that await those who do harm to one of God's little ones (verse 42). The warning is stark and the imagery is vivid. It is better to drown in the sea wearing a millstone as a collar than to experience the fate of one who causes a person weak in faith to stumble and sin. Jesus continues his warning in the next three sayings by focusing on personal stumbling and the causes of sin that arise within oneself (verses 43–47). Jesus is not advocating self-mutila-tion of our hand, foot, and eye, because it is not these body parts that cause us to sin. But just as a surgeon would remove a body part in order to save a life, it is better to make any sacrifice, no matter how costly, than to lose eternal life. Jesus uses graphic hyperbole to teach that we should radically remove any sin-ful enticements and selfish attachments that imperil our eternal destiny.

Each of these sayings of Jesus contrasts the two possible destinies resulting from God's final judgment: the kingdom of God or the fires of hell. In the age to come, we will fully enter the eternity we have chosen for ourselves. Jesus depicts hell using words from the last verse of Isaiah, describing those who rebel against God: "for their worm shall not die, their fire shall not be quenched, and they shall be an abhorrence to all flesh" (Isa 66:24). These images describe in figurative language the anguish of eternal separation from God. With every decision and action over the course of our lifetime we orient ourselves either to heaven or hell, eternal life with God or eternal alienation from him, and at death we embrace what has truly become our choice.

Jesus' final teaching offers three sayings concerning salt, which was used in the ancient world both as a preservative and a seasoning. It seems that salt here refers to the commitment and fervor that genuine discipleship requires. Being "salted with fire" means purified through the trials and testing that come with discipleship. Disciples must maintain their "saltiness," lest they lose their zeal and their ability to attract others to the gospel. But if disciples main-tain their fervent commitment and love for Christ, they will be brought to peace and unity with one another.

Reflection and discussion

• Jesus said, "Whoever is not against us is for us" (verse 40). What might be some of the implications of Jesus' proverb for modern disciples and for the church today?

• Disunity, jealousy, and competition hinder the spread of the gospel. How can Christians of different denominations collaborate and work together for the sake of Jesus Christ?

• What four things does Jesus say are "better"? What is the purpose of his graphic hyperbole?

• Do some of the standards Jesus holds for his disciples seem impossible for me? To what degree am I willing to let Jesus redirect my life?

Prayer

Jesus Messiah, I want you to be the Lord of my life. Teach me to value the things that really matter and to align the goals of my life with your will for me. Help me to choose you in all things and orient my life toward the fullness of your eternal kingdom.

SUGGESTIONS FOR FACILITATORS, GROUP SESSION 2

1. If there are newcomers who were not present for the first group session, introduce them now.

2. You may want to pray this prayer as a group:

Father of our Lord Jesus Christ, you revealed your Son to his disciples on the mountain of Transfiguration and along the way that leads to the cross. Although we want to remain with Jesus on the mountain, he shows us the way of disciple-ship along the road to Jerusalem. Teach us to deny ourselves, to become the servants of all, to take up the cross, and to follow Jesus wherever he leads. As we continue to study, reflect, and pray with the gospel of Mark, send us your Spirit to guide and direct us.

3. Ask one or more of the following questions:
   • What was your biggest challenge in Bible study over this past week?
   • What did you learn about yourself this week?

4. Discuss lessons 1 through 6 together. Assuming that group members have read the Scripture and commentary during the week, there is no need to read the lessons aloud. As you review each lesson, you might want to briefly sum-marize the Scripture passages of each lesson and ask the group what stands out most clearly from the commentary.

5. Choose one or more of the questions for reflection and discussion from each lesson to talk over as a group. You may want to ask group members which question was most challenging or helpful to them as you review each lesson.

6. Keep the discussion moving, but don't rush the discussion in order to com-plete more questions. Allow time for the questions that provoke the most discussion.

7. Instruct group members to complete lessons 7 through 12 on their own during the six days before the next group meeting. They should write out their own answers to the questions as preparation for next week's group discussion.

8. Conclude by praying aloud together the prayer at the end of lesson 6, or any other prayer you choose.

"So they are no longer two, but one flesh.
Therefore what God has joined together, let no one separate."

Mark 10:8–9

Teaching on
Marriage and Divorce

MARK 10:1–12   ¹*He left that place and went to the region of Judea and beyond the Jordan. And crowds again gathered around him; and, as was his custom, he again taught them.*

²*Some Pharisees came, and to test him they asked, "Is it lawful for a man to divorce his wife?" ³He answered them, "What did Moses command you?" ⁴They said, "Moses allowed a man to write a certificate of dismissal and to divorce her." ⁵But Jesus said to them, "Because of your hardness of heart he wrote this commandment for you. ⁶But from the beginning of creation, 'God made them male and female.' ⁷For this reason a man shall leave his father and mother and be joined to his wife, ⁸and the two shall become one flesh.' So they are no longer two, but one flesh. ⁹Therefore what God has joined together, let no one separate."*

¹⁰*Then in the house the disciples asked him again about this matter. ¹¹He said to them, "Whoever divorces his wife and marries another commits adultery against her; ¹²and if she divorces her husband and marries another, she commits adultery."*

A s Jesus continues to travel with his disciples into Judea and toward Jerusalem, he continues to teach them about the implications of the radical choice of being his follower. Although crowds continue to gather around him to listen to his teaching, Jesus focuses his instruction on the practical aspects of being a disciple in everyday life and expands on his teachings with his disciples in private. Mark narrates Jesus' teachings on marriage, raising children, and dealing with financial success and wealth, making it clear that the values of God's kingdom are quite different than the values of the culture of the time.

Again, some Pharisees come to Jesus with a question designed to entrap him: "Is it lawful for a man to divorce his wife?" Behind the question lay the dangerous political issue of Herod's marriage to Herodias, who had divorced her husband to marry him. John the Baptist's criticism of this marriage had ended in his beheading, so the Pharisees thought this might be an easy way to ensnare Jesus.

In response to Jesus' counter question, "What did Moses command you?" the Pharisees state that the Torah allows a man to write a certificate of divorce "if she does not please him because he finds something objectionable about her" (Deut 24:1). There was much debate within Judaism over the meaning of the "something objectionable" that would justify divorce. Jesus demonstrates, however, that their focus on what God allows due to the hardness of the human heart is misguided.

Jesus states that God's original intention for marriage should be the center of their attention. This divine purpose is best expressed in the creation accounts, describing how God made them male and female so that they could join themselves together as "one flesh" (verse 8).

This communion of love between a husband and wife points to God's ultimate purpose in creating humanity in his image. Since God himself has created their bond, what God has joined together no human being may separate through divorce (verse 9). With the coming of God's kingdom, humanity has been given a new power to experience and live what God intended from the beginning.

As has happened several times before, Jesus' disciples are confused and question him when they are alone with him away from the crowd. His teaching is quite remarkable, so his disciples want to make sure that he said what they think he said. In ancient Israel a man was considered an adulterer when he had a sexual relationship with a married woman, in which case he was guilty of adultery against the husband of this woman, not his wife. But if a woman had a sexual relationship with another man, she was guilty of adultery against her husband. This reflected the view that a woman was in some sense the property of her husband. Jesus teaches, however, that what is adultery for one is adultery for the other, and that the sin of adultery is a sin against one's husband or wife. If a man dismisses his wife in favor of another, he commits adultery against his wife; and if a woman divorces her husband and marries another, she commits adultery against her husband. In this way, Jesus implicitly teaches that there is a basic equality between men and women in marriage and that each belongs to the other.

Jesus' teaching on the permanence of marriage was difficult for his first disciples, and it is difficult for the church today. It is no accident that Mark placed this teaching in the section concerned with the cost of discipleship. Jesus calls husbands and wives to cultivate selfless love in order to maintain the commitment necessary for their marriage to endure. While the church continues to teach and uphold the ideal of Jesus, it also practices the compassion of Jesus in helping people who cannot live up to the ideal of marriage, due to abuse, abandonment, or other factors. In carrying out the values of Jesus, the church seeks to help people prepare for marriage, to strengthen them in the struggles of marriage, and to support them in cases in which marriage cannot be maintained.

Reflection and discussion

• How were the Pharisees trying to test Jesus by their question about divorce?

• What is the reason for Jesus' teaching on the permanence of marriage?

• In what ways does Jesus' teaching stress the equality and mutual belonging of a husband and wife in marriage?

• How does this teaching encourage the church to help prepare couples for marriage and support them through the struggles of marriage?

Prayer

Lord Jesus, in the daily challenges of marriage and family life we find the most opportunities to put into practice your teachings on self-denial, humility and service. Strengthen me in my commitments and in my struggles to live out your design for human love.

"Let the little children come to me; do not stop them; for it is to
such as these that the kingdom of God belongs." Mark 10:14

Jesus Embraces and Blesses the Children

MARK 10:13–16 ¹³*People were bringing little children to him in order that
he might touch them; and the disciples spoke sternly to them.* ¹⁴*But when Jesus
saw this, he was indignant and said to them, "Let the little children come to me;
do not stop them; for it is to such as these that the kingdom of God belongs.*
¹⁵*Truly I tell you, whoever does not receive the kingdom of God as a little child
will never enter it." * ¹⁶*And he took them up in his arms, laid his hands on them,
and blessed them.*

Jesus' discussion of marriage naturally leads into a teaching centering on
children. He demonstrates his tender love for children as he encourages
parents to bring their children to him to embrace and bless. The word
translated as "children" includes those up to twelve years of age. Again Jesus acts
contrary to the accepted values of his day in which children had no legal rights
or social status. Children were to be neither seen nor heard in public matters.

No reason is given as to why the disciples tried to prevent parents from
bringing their children to Jesus. Perhaps they thought that the children would
be distracting and disruptive. But Jesus forbade anyone to hinder the parents

from bringing their children to him. This is the only passage in the gospels in which Jesus is described as "indignant," a term indicating outrage at an offense. He indicates in the strongest possible terms his desire that the children be given access to him. He commands, "Let the little children come to me; do not stop them" (verse 14).

In the early centuries of the church, this passage was used to support the practice of baptizing infants and children. Jesus says, "for it is to such as these that the kingdom of God belongs." Though baptism might not have been the original reason for Jesus' welcome of the children, his love for them and his free and undeserved bestowal of God's kingdom to all certainly seem to support the welcome of infants and children into the life of God's kingdom through the free and undeserved gift of Christian baptism.

But Jesus is not just speaking about children here, for he says that God's kingdom belongs "to such as these." People who are like these children enter into the reign of God. What does it mean to be like children in readiness for the kingdom? Children receive gifts with humility, not thinking that they are deserving of the gifts; for them, all depends on the goodness of the giver. To receive the precious gift of the kingdom as a little child means that the recipient obtains the gift now in simplicity and trust, experiencing its first fruits through God's Spirit. But that recipient must wait in hope for the full experience of that gift, the consummation of God's kingdom in the age to come.

The episode ends with Jesus holding the children in his arms, laying his hands on their heads, and blessing them. These final actions indicate that the passage is not just about those who are "like" children, but also about the special love of Jesus toward children. Jesus' embrace of these children serves as an image for what God wants to do for us through Jesus, and the children receiving his embrace provides an image for our receiving the kingdom of God.

Reflection and discussion

• What are the qualities of children that make entrance into the kingdom of God possible for us?

• Why did the early church use this passage to support the baptism of infants and children along with their parents?

• In what ways is entering the kingdom of God the same as entering into relationship with Jesus?

• What can I do to become more childlike in my openness to God's reign today? What might be blocking my receptiveness to God's kingdom?

Prayer

Loving Lord, you have offered me the gift of God's kingdom to be experienced now and completely in the future. Give me the qualities of trust, simplicity, and gratitude so that I might receive this precious gift from you.

"Children, how hard it is to enter the kingdom of God!
It is easier for a camel to go through the eye of a needle than
for someone who is rich to enter the kingdom of God."

Mark 10:24–25

Teaching on
Riches and Possessions

MARK 10:17–31 ¹⁷*As he was setting out on a journey, a man ran up and knelt before him, and asked him, "Good Teacher, what must I do to inherit eternal life?"* ¹⁸*Jesus said to him, "Why do you call me good? No one is good but God alone.* ¹⁹*You know the commandments: 'You shall not murder; You shall not commit adultery; You shall not steal; You shall not bear false witness; You shall not defraud; Honor your father and mother.'"* ²⁰*He said to him, "Teacher, I have kept all these since my youth."* ²¹*Jesus, looking at him, loved him and said, "You lack one thing; go, sell what you own, and give the money to the poor, and you will have treasure in heaven; then come, follow me."* ²²*When he heard this, he was shocked and went away grieving, for he had many possessions.*

²³*Then Jesus looked around and said to his disciples, "How hard it will be for those who have wealth to enter the kingdom of God!"* ²⁴*And the disciples were perplexed at these words. But Jesus said to them again, "Children, how hard it is to enter the kingdom of God!* ²⁵*It is easier for a camel to go through the eye of a needle than for someone who is rich to enter the kingdom of God."* ²⁶*They were greatly astounded and said to one another, "Then who can be saved?"* ²⁷*Jesus*

41

looked at them and said, "For mortals it is impossible, but not for God; for God all things are possible."

28 Peter began to say to him, "Look, we have left everything and followed you." 29 Jesus said, "Truly I tell you, there is no one who has left house or brothers or sisters or mother or father or children or fields, for my sake and for the sake of the good news, 30 who will not receive a hundredfold now in this age—houses, brothers and sisters, mothers and children, and fields, with persecutions—and in the age to come eternal life. 31 But many who are first will be last, and the last will be first."

As Jesus continues his journey toward Jerusalem, his teachings continue to focus on what it means to be a disciple. The man who runs up and kneels before Jesus clearly has an urgent question burning on his heart, and he recognizes that Jesus can meet his deepest need. The man addresses Jesus as "Good Teacher" and asks Jesus how he can inherit eternal life. The various expressions used in this passage—"inheriting eternal life" (verse 17), "having treasure in heaven" (verse 21), "entering the kingdom of God" (verse 23), and "being saved" (verse 26)—are all different ways of expressing the fullness of life that Jesus has come to give to those who choose to receive it.

Jesus' response to the man sounds puzzling, and its meaning is disputed by commentators: "Why do you call me good? No one is good but God alone" (verse 18). Jesus is not denying his own goodness; rather, he is challenging the man to consider why and on what basis he calls Jesus good. Yes, Jesus is a wise teacher and a compassionate healer. But ultimately goodness belongs to God alone. Can the man recognize in Jesus that infinite goodness which can satisfy the deep longing of his heart? If the man is able to recognize the divine goodness of Jesus, he can receive the gift of life that he so urgently seeks.

But unfortunately the man exemplifies the opposite of what Jesus has just described as characteristic of children. His wealth prevents him from accepting God's gift with simplicity and trust. Jesus recognizes that the "one thing" the man lacks is detachment from his "many possessions" (verses 21–22). The rich man thinks that he can earn the gift of eternal life by following all the commandments, and he is unable to humbly receive the gift of God's kingdom. When Jesus commands him to sell his possessions, give the money to the poor, and then come follow, the wealthy man "was shocked and went away grieving." He is unable to dispense with the one thing that is obstructing his ability to accept the gift of eternal life. Though called to discipleship by Jesus, the man turns away rather than follow Jesus.

Jesus uses an unforgettable hyperbole to describe the obstacle that riches pose for those who seek entry into God's kingdom (verse 25). The camel was the largest animal in Palestine, and the eye of a needle was the smallest opening in a familiar object. Jesus tells his disciples that the attractions of wealth and possessions are so alluring that a rich person, with his or her own might, is unable to sever its grasp. Just as it is impossible for a camel to crawl through a needle's eye, depending on riches, privilege, and security creates an insurmountable obstacle to sharing in the kingdom.

Like most Jews of Jesus' day, the disciples assume that wealth is a sign of God's favor, and so they are "greatly astonished" at this maxim of Jesus (verse 26). If those who enjoy God's favor find it so difficult to enter God's kingdom, then how can anyone "be saved"? Jesus' answer implies that it is impossible from a human standpoint to overcome the powerful lure of wealth and to be dependent on God alone. The process of being saved, the transformation that comes through following Jesus, is impossible for human beings to achieve on their own, "but for God all things are possible" (verse 27). Just as God has given us mortal life as a gift, God can save us from sin and death and give us eternal life.

Reflection and discussion

• How could this man's riches prevent him from following Jesus and block his way to eternal life?

• In what sense does Jesus teach that it is "impossible" to earn the kingdom of God?

• In what ways do my possessions possess me? How can material wealth lead to spiritual complacency?

• What do I need to leave behind in order to deepen my commitment to following Jesus?

Prayer

Lord Jesus, you invite me to detach myself from the lure of temporal securities, worldly influence, and material wealth in order to follow you. Give me the security of your grace, the influence of your Spirit, and the riches of your kingdom.

> "See, we are going up to Jerusalem, and the Son of Man
> will be handed over to the chief priests and the scribes,
> and they will condemn him to death."
>
> Mark 10:33

On the Way to Jerusalem

MARK 10:32–34 ³²*They were on the road, going up to Jerusalem, and Jesus was walking ahead of them; they were amazed, and those who followed were afraid. He took the twelve aside again and began to tell them what was to happen to him,* ³³*saying, "See, we are going up to Jerusalem, and the Son of Man will be handed over to the chief priests and the scribes, and they will condemn him to death; then they will hand him over to the Gentiles;* ³⁴*they will mock him, and spit upon him, and flog him, and kill him; and after three days he will rise again."*

Jesus continues to travel with his disciples. This time the gospel specifically notes that they were "going up to Jerusalem." From whichever direction one is traveling, the way to Jerusalem is always "up"—up to Mount Zion where God's temple is located. Jesus most likely traveled to Jerusalem many times during his life, but Mark's gospel mentions only this one time to emphasize its significance as the end of Jesus' journey to the cross. Here Jesus will fulfill his destiny as the suffering Messiah.

The text notes that "Jesus was walking ahead of them," emphasizing his sense of determination and his firm desire to do the will of the Father. Although he knows what awaits him there, Jesus resolutely proceeds to Jerusalem. The text also notes that Jesus' disciples are "amazed," a response previously associated with a sense of astonishment at what Jesus had said. But now, their amazement involves Jesus' firm resolve and sense of destiny. His desire to fulfill God's will evokes a sense of reverential awe in those who were traveling with him.

For his closest disciples, the final leg of Jesus' journey evokes fear. They know that Jesus has powerful enemies there, and they are afraid of what will happen to both Jesus and themselves. But Jesus does not dismiss their fears; he once again takes them aside and provides them with private teaching concerning his approaching passion. This third and final prophecy of his death and resurrection is the most solemn and detailed. In fact, it is more of a preview and synopsis of the coming passion account.

Referring to himself again as the Son of Man, Jesus tells his disciples that he will be "handed over" (verse 33). He will be handed over through the betrayal of Judas to the religious authorities. These will then hand over Jesus to the Gentiles, the non-Jewish Roman authorities. Yet, on the divine level, the action expresses God's redemptive purpose in handing over his Son to sinful humanity. Jesus' direct and precise prediction of his coming passion indicates that he knew full well and with exact detail his approaching death. This was no tragic accident, but rather a divine necessity. Jesus continued on the way to Jerusalem because he desired to fulfill the Father's loving will for humanity and to complete his redemptive plan.

This is the first indication of two distinct groups involved in the passion of Jesus. The first is the Jewish leaders, who are clearly distinguished from the Jewish people as a whole. These chief priests and scribes will condemn Jesus to death and then hand him over. The second is the Gentiles, that is, the Roman authorities led by Pontius Pilate. These Gentiles will mock him, spit upon him, flog him, and kill him. These humiliating details will be fulfilled to the letter in the passion account. Yet, all of these gruesome details will conclude with a glorious victory over death itself.

Reflection and discussion

• Why did Jesus repeatedly tell his disciples that he was going to suffer, be put to death, and rise again?

• In what sense were the followers of Jesus both amazed and afraid as Jesus walked ahead of them to Jerusalem?

• How does Mark's gospel highlight the fact that the way of discipleship is the way of suffering, dying, and rising—following Jesus who has led the way?

Prayer

Suffering Messiah, you lead the way as disciples follow you up to Jerusalem and toward your cross. Help me to follow you along the way of the cross, prepared for suffering, betrayal, and ridicule, so that I will share in the life you have promised.

"Whoever wishes to become great among you
must be your servant, and whoever wishes to be first among you
must be slave of all." Mark 10:43–44

Following the Suffering Servant

MARK 10:35–45 ³⁵*James and John, the sons of Zebedee, came forward to him and said to him, "Teacher, we want you to do for us whatever we ask of you."* ³⁶*And he said to them, "What is it you want me to do for you?"* ³⁷*And they said to him, "Grant us to sit, one at your right hand and one at your left, in your glory."* ³⁸*But Jesus said to them, "You do not know what you are asking. Are you able to drink the cup that I drink, or be baptized with the baptism that I am baptized with?"* ³⁹*They replied, "We are able." Then Jesus said to them, "The cup that I drink you will drink; and with the baptism with which I am baptized, you will be baptized;* ⁴⁰*but to sit at my right hand or at my left is not mine to grant, but it is for those for whom it has been prepared."*

⁴¹*When the ten heard this, they began to be angry with James and John.* ⁴²*So Jesus called them and said to them, "You know that among the Gentiles those whom they recognize as their rulers lord it over them, and their great ones are tyrants over them.* ⁴³*But it is not so among you; but whoever wishes to become great among you must be your servant,* ⁴⁴*and whoever wishes to be first among you must be slave of all.* ⁴⁵*For the Son of Man came not to be served but to serve, and to give his life a ransom for many."*

The third and final prediction of Jesus' passion is followed again by an example of failure on the part of the disciples. The indirect way in which the two disciples make their appeal to Jesus indicates that they realize its brazenness. They do not reveal the specific nature of their request until Jesus asks them directly, "What is it you want me to do for you?" (verse 36). It is almost as if James and John had not heard the description of Jesus' suffering and death. Their request to sit at the right and left of Jesus when he is enthroned in Jerusalem indicates a concern only for their own power and prestige.

Like Peter, Jesus' other two closest disciples discern correctly that Jesus is the Messiah, but they completely fail to understand the implications of this title for Jesus and for themselves. The tactless request of James and John shows that they refuse to accept Jesus' repeated teaching concerning his coming passion. They are imagining their own future prominence and, like Peter, fail to realize that Jesus is the suffering Messiah who is leading his disciples to Jerusalem, not to experience earthly glory but for the sake of the cross.

Jesus' response reinforces his passion prediction and the role of his disciples in his suffering (verse 38). In the prophets and psalms, "the cup" is a metaphor for what God has in store for someone: either the cup of blessing or the cup of his wrath. Here, the cup expresses God's judgment on sin which Jesus will take upon himself at the cross. Immersion in water is also a biblical metaphor for both cleansing renewal and devastating calamity. Here, baptism refers to the overwhelming suffering that Jesus will endure. James and John think that perhaps the cup and the baptism simply refer to fellowship with Jesus, so in response to the question of Jesus about whether they can drink the cup and be baptized with Jesus, they glibly respond, "We are able" (verse 39). Yet, Jesus is asking his disciples if they are willing to be united with him in redemptive suffering. Only after the cross do the two disciples understand Jesus' response, as they realize that those at the right hand and left hand of the Messiah are the two bandits crucified with him (15:27).

The angry response of the other ten toward James and John implicates the Twelve in their selfish blunder. The others are upset that James and John have upstaged them because they too desire special places of honor in the kingdom. Their failure in discipleship offers Jesus the opening to again offer a teaching on true greatness in the kingdom of God. After reminding the disciples of how the Roman tyrants throw their weight around and enjoy their perks at the expense of their subjects, Jesus emphatically states, "But it is not so among you" (verses 42–43). In Christian leadership there is no place for rivalry, self-promotion, and domination over others. The way to true greatness in the kingdom is through self-sacrifice for others, humbly caring for their needs and putting oneself at their service.

Jesus concludes his teaching by offering his own life as a model for leadership in his church and summarizing the purpose of his mission as Messiah: "For the Son of Man came not to be served but to serve, and to give his life a ransom for many" (verse 45). Jesus was sent by the Father not for his own advantage, but to give his life to rescue others. As God ransomed his people from slavery in Egypt, Jesus came to ransom the human race from the bondage of sin and death. In his passion Jesus would pay the price, the infinite value of his own life, in exchange for us. The term "for many" expresses a vast multitude that excludes no one. Jesus' description of his mission identifies himself with the Suffering Servant of Isaiah's prophecy, who is "wounded for our transgressions, crushed for our iniquities" (Isa 53:5), making his life "an offering for sin" (Isa 53:10). Although the Suffering Servant pours out his life and is counted among criminals, "yet he bore the sins of many, and made intercession for the transgressors" (Isa 53:12). The suffering and death of Jesus as "a ransom for many" is not only the supreme example of loving service but the sacrifice by which he has redeemed the world.

Reflection and discussion

• How were Peter, James, and John able to state clearly who Jesus is but fail to understand his mission and its implications for their own lives? How might the same be said of me?

• In what ways might Jesus' words about the cup and the baptism allude to the church's sacraments of Eucharist and baptism? In what ways do these sacraments unite disciples in the death and resurrection of Jesus?

• In what ways does the suffering servant prophecy of Isaiah describe the mission of Jesus?

• Who are examples to me of generous service to others? What is my understanding of greatness in the church and in the world?

Prayer

Suffering Messiah, help me to give myself in service of others and unite my sufferings with yours. I want to follow you, knowing the consequences of faithful discipleship and confident that you are with me along the way.

Jesus said to him, "Go; your faith has made you well."
Immediately he regained his sight and followed him on the way.

Mark 10:52

Bartimaeus Receives His Sight and Follows Jesus

MARK 10:46–52 *46 They came to Jericho. As he and his disciples and a large crowd were leaving Jericho, Bartimaeus son of Timaeus, a blind beggar, was sitting by the roadside. 47 When he heard that it was Jesus of Nazareth, he began to shout out and say, "Jesus, Son of David, have mercy on me!" 48 Many sternly ordered him to be quiet, but he cried out even more loudly, "Son of David, have mercy on me!" 49 Jesus stood still and said, "Call him here." And they called the blind man, saying to him, "Take heart; get up, he is calling you." 50 So throwing off his cloak, he sprang up and came to Jesus. 51 Then Jesus said to him, "What do you want me to do for you?" The blind man said to him, "My teacher, let me see again." 52 Jesus said to him, "Go; your faith has made you well." Immediately he regained his sight and followed him on the way.*

The healing of Bartimaeus is the final healing miracle of Mark's gospel and concludes the long middle section of the gospel. This section began with Jesus healing another blind man before his long journey toward his destiny in Jerusalem. These two miracles of sight serve as bookends to bracket this segment of the gospel in which Jesus teaches about his coming passion and about the path of discipleship. The first healing of a blind man was a gradual, two-stage healing at Bethsaida; now, at the end of the journey, this healing of the blind man is instantaneous and complete. Mark has framed the journey of Jesus in this way to symbolize Jesus gradually healing the blindness of his disciples through his teaching and example along "the way." Jericho is the last stop on the southward journey of Jesus before climbing the steep road to his destiny in Jerusalem. At this point the vision of the disciples is still only partial; only with the death and resurrection of Jesus will their eyes be fully opened.

As Jesus and his disciples leave Jericho, they are accompanied by a large crowd of pilgrims headed to Jerusalem for the feast of Passover. Bartimaeus, the blind begger, has strategically positioned himself along the way so that he can beg for alms from the passing pilgrims. His sitting by the roadside, in contrast to the festive crowd that walks along, emphasizes his disability and social isolation. When he hears that Jesus is passing by, he shouts, "Jesus, Son of David, have mercy on me!" (verses 47–48). The title Son of David acknowledges that Jesus is the royal Messiah, the descendant of King David who would bring the kingdom and rule over Israel forever. Bartimaus was poor, needy, blind, and helpless, yet he had an unrelenting trust in Jesus as the Messiah. His example of faith is a strong contrast to the self-sufficient rich man and to the ambitions of James and John.

The response of Bartimaeus to the call of Jesus is a model of enthusiastic and expectant faith. He throws off his cloak, springs up, and comes to Jesus (verse 50). Jesus' question to Bartimaeus is the same question he had asked James and John: "What do you want me to do for you?" (verse 51). The sons of Zebedee wanted honor and power, but the blind man replies simply, "My teacher, let me see again." Like children and those childlike ones who receive the kingdom humbly and trustingly, Bartimaeus displays the faith that heals and saves. He is not only healed from his physical blindness, but he receives the insight and faith to understand Jesus and to be his disciple. The account concludes by telling us that Bartimaeus followed Jesus "on the way" (verse 52). This means not only that Bartimaeus followed the crowd up to Jerusalem with Jesus, but that he followed on the way of discipleship. Unlike the closest disciples of Jesus, Bartimaeus sees clearly because he knows who Jesus is and what it means to be his disciple on the way of the cross.

Reflection and discussion

• On a map of first-century Palestine, trace the route of Jesus and his disciples from Caesarea Philippi, to Capernaum, to Jericho, and up to Jerusalem. How does Mark's gospel use this journey to teach the way of discipleship?

• Jesus asks me too, "What do you want me to do for you?" How do I respond to him?

• In what ways is Bartimaeus a model for discipleship? How is his response to Jesus more complete than that of the rich man or of James and John?

Prayer

Jesus, Son of David, have mercy on me! You have led me on the journey to Jerusalem as you healed my blindness and my resistance to being your disciple. Help me respond to your call with confident and joyful faith.

SUGGESTIONS FOR FACILITATORS, GROUP SESSION 3

1. Welcome group members and ask if there are any announcements anyone would like to make.

2. You may want to pray this prayer as a group:

Creating and Redeeming God, you have shown us how to be disciples of your Son, Jesus, as we follow him on the way that leads to the cross. Detach us from the lure of material wealth, temporal securities, and worldly influence in order to free us to receive your grace. Give us humility, trust, and gratitude so that we may receive the gift of your kingdom with an open heart. As disciples of your Suffering Servant, let us unite our afflictions with his and give ourselves in service of others. May we respond to his call with confident and joyful faith.

3. Ask one or more of the following questions:
   - Which image from the lessons this week stands out most memorably to you?
   - What is the most important lesson you learned through your study this week?

4. Discuss lessons 7 through 12. Choose one or more of the questions for reflection and discussion from each lesson to discuss as a group. You may want to ask group members which question was most challenging or helpful to them as you review each lesson.

5. Remember that there are no definitive answers for these discussion questions. The insights of group members will add to the understanding of all. None of these questions require an expert.

6. After talking about each lesson, instruct group members to complete lessons 13 through 18 on their own during the six days before the next group meeting. They should write out their own answers to the questions as preparation for next week's group discussion.

7. Ask the group if anyone is having any particular problems with the Bible study during the week. You may want to share advice and encouragement within the group.

8. Conclude by praying aloud together the prayer at the end of one of the lessons discussed. You may add to the prayer based on the sharing that has occurred in the group.

"Hosanna! Blessed is the one who comes in the name of the Lord!
Blessed is the coming kingdom of our ancestor David!
Hosanna in the highest heaven!"

Mark 11:9–10

The Messiah
Enters Jerusalem

MARK 11:1–11 ^{1}*When they were approaching Jerusalem, at Bethphage and Bethany, near the Mount of Olives, he sent two of his disciples ^{2}and said to them, "Go into the village ahead of you, and immediately as you enter it, you will find tied there a colt that has never been ridden; untie it and bring it. ^{3}If anyone says to you, 'Why are you doing this?' just say this, 'The Lord needs it and will send it back here immediately.'" ^{4}They went away and found a colt tied near a door, outside in the street. As they were untying it, ^{5}some of the bystanders said to them, "What are you doing, untying the colt?" ^{6}They told them what Jesus had said; and they allowed them to take it. ^{7}Then they brought the colt to Jesus and threw their cloaks on it; and he sat on it. ^{8}Many people spread their cloaks on the road, and others spread leafy branches that they had cut in the fields. ^{9}Then those who went ahead and those who followed were shouting,*

"Hosanna!

Blessed is the one who comes in the name of the Lord!

^{10}Blessed is the coming kingdom of our ancestor David!

Hosanna in the highest heaven!"

¹¹*Then he entered Jerusalem and went into the temple; and when he had looked around at everything, as it was already late, he went out to Bethany with the twelve.*

The final section of Mark's gospel takes place in the space of eight days, from what the early church celebrated as Palm Sunday to Easter Sunday. By the fourth century, these events had been organized into the liturgy of Passion Week for remembering the saving events of Jesus' final days in Jerusalem. These episodes can be divided into two main parts: first, Jesus' entry into Jerusalem followed by his actions and teachings centered on the temple (Mark 11–13), and second, Jesus' passion, death, and resurrection (Mark 14–16).

Jesus has come to the climactic stage in his resolute journey to Jerusalem. As Jesus ascended to the city from Jericho, he would have passed by the village of Bethany, less than two miles east of Jerusalem, and then the village of Bethphage, on the eastern slope of the Mount of Olives. The western slope of the Mount of Olives faces Jerusalem and provides a panoramic view of the city. As he approaches the holy city, Jesus arranges for his entry into Jerusalem as a conscious messianic act. He will travel down the slopes of the Mount of Olives, across the Kidron Valley, and then enter the temple precincts through its eastern gate.

The careful preparations for Jesus' entry point to its deeply symbolic significance. He will ride into the city on a young donkey, "a colt that has never been ridden" (verse 2). The virginal nature of the colt, one that has never been ridden, follows biblical stipulations that an animal devoted to a sacred purpose must be one that has not previously been put to any ordinary use. For example, the ark of the covenant was transported by two cows "that have never borne a yoke" (1 Sam 6:7). This is related also to the tradition that Jesus was born from a virgin womb, that had never borne a child, and was buried in a virgin tomb, that had never before contained a corpse.

Jesus' triumphal entry into the city is an enactment of Zechariah's prophecy: "Rejoice greatly, O daughter Zion! Shout aloud, O daughter Jerusalem! Lo, your king comes to you; triumphant and victorious is he, humble and riding on a donkey, on a colt, the foal of a donkey" (Zech 9:9). Israel's Messiah enters the city not with a display of military might and political power as most were expecting. He comes to his people not on a war horse like the generals of the time, but on a lowly donkey, in humility and peace.

Many spread their cloaks and leafy branches on the road as a sign of homage. The crowd chants from Psalm 118, one of the pilgrimage hymns sung by the people as they entered the temple for a festival. "Hosanna" is a Hebrew word meaning "save now!" The cry asks God "in the highest heaven" to come and save his people. The psalm expresses hope in the coming Messiah, but does not directly acknowledge Jesus as the Son of David in whom the kingdom has come. Mark, however, knows that his readers have come to realize that Jesus' true identity is expressed in the people's acclamation, an understanding that will be acknowledged by his disciples after his death and resurrection.

The narrative ends anticlimactically as Jesus enters Jerusalem and the temple. Since the hour is late, Jesus' scrutiny of the area of the temple forebodes the judgment to come. The triumphal scene will soon turn to tragedy. The crowd's excited shouts of "Hosanna" will turn to shouts of "Crucify him!" As in the liturgy of Palm Sunday, the joyful procession is only a prelude for the proclamation of the passion.

Reflection and discussion

• Why does Jesus enter Jerusalem on a colt that has never been ridden?

• What does Jesus' manner of entering Jerusalem say about his character and his mission?

• What does the acclamation from Psalm 118 tell me about Jesus? Why do we chant these words at the beginning of the liturgy's Eucharistic Prayer?

• How does the people's shout, "Hosanna," express their deep longings for God?

• What is the difference between emotional fervor and genuine faith? Why is one sometimes mistaken for the other?

Prayer

Son of David, you are the royal Messiah who enters your holy city in humility. As I welcome you into my heart with joyful acclamations, give me a genuine faith to receive God's kingdom which you have come to bring.

Jesus was teaching and saying, "Is it not written,
'My house shall be called a house of prayer for all the nations'?
But you have made it a den of robbers."

Mark 11:17

Judgment of the Fig Tree and the Temple

MARK 11:12–25 *¹²On the following day, when they came from Bethany, he was hungry. ¹³Seeing in the distance a fig tree in leaf, he went to see whether perhaps he would find anything on it. When he came to it, he found nothing but leaves, for it was not the season for figs. ¹⁴He said to it, "May no one ever eat fruit from you again." And his disciples heard it.*

¹⁵Then they came to Jerusalem. And he entered the temple and began to drive out those who were selling and those who were buying in the temple, and he overturned the tables of the money changers and the seats of those who sold doves; ¹⁶and he would not allow anyone to carry anything through the temple. ¹⁷He was teaching and saying, "Is it not written,

'My house shall be called a house of prayer for all the nations'?

But you have made it a den of robbers."

¹⁸And when the chief priests and the scribes heard it, they kept looking for a way to kill him; for they were afraid of him, because the whole crowd was spellbound by his teaching. ¹⁹And when evening came, Jesus and his disciples went out of the city.

²⁰*In the morning as they passed by, they saw the fig tree withered away to its roots.* ²¹*Then Peter remembered and said to him, "Rabbi, look! The fig tree that you cursed has withered."* ²²*Jesus answered them, "Have faith in God.* ²³*Truly I tell you, if you say to this mountain, 'Be taken up and thrown into the sea,' and if you do not doubt in your heart, but believe that what you say will come to pass, it will be done for you.* ²⁴*So I tell you, whatever you ask for in prayer, believe that you have received it, and it will be yours.*

²⁵*"Whenever you stand praying, forgive, if you have anything against anyone; so that your Father in heaven may also forgive you your trespasses."*

The next day Jesus performs more symbolic actions, like his entrance into Jerusalem the day before. The judgment of the barren fig tree and the cleansing of the temple are both acted-out parables that must be pondered to discover their obscure meaning. Mark's explanatory note, that "it was not the season for figs," lets the reader know that what Jesus is doing is not about the fig tree at all. In the writings of the prophets, the fig tree is frequently used as a symbol for announcing God's judgment upon his people. In the writings of Micah, God laments that he finds no fruit to eat on the vines of his people: "There is no first-ripe fig for which I hunger" (Mic 7:1). Jesus searches in vain for the fruit of covenant fidelity in the city, but finds only injustice. The temple practices had become all leaf and no fruit, only ceremonial foliage and nothing that gave real nourishment and life.

Mark's method of sandwiching the cleansing of the temple between the two parts of the fig tree incident shows that the two accounts interpret one another. Jesus' judgment of the fig tree, "May no one ever eat fruit from you again" (verse 14), and Peter's subsequent observation, "The fig tree that you cursed has withered" (verse 21), serve as an interpretive guide for understanding Jesus' cleansing of the temple. The tree's absence of fruit signifies the lack of faith and prayer that Jesus finds in the temple. His cursing of the fig tree and its withering away to its roots is a prophetic signal that the worship and sacrifices offered in the temple, with all their elaborate splendor, are drawing to an end and the temple will soon be destroyed.

Jesus' dramatic action in the temple was performed in the covered portico around the perimeter of the temple grounds, the area of the temple called the Court of the Gentiles. Here tables were set up for the exchange of foreign money so that Jews could pay the annual temple tax. Merchants were selling animals to facilitate the offering of blemish-free sacrifices, including doves which were the sacrifices of the poor. Although these were necessary services for the temple offerings, there were other places in the city and on the Mount of Olives where such transactions took place. The exchanges in the temple area were set up by the priestly families and became quite profitable endeavors. Jesus was not attacking the temple and its system of sacrifices; rather, he was assailing its abuses, the corruption and commercialism he found there. Jesus' action was directed against those selling and buying and also against those who were carrying things through the temple courts, as if the sacred precincts could be used for a shortcut (verses 15–16).

The reasons for Jesus' prophetic action can be discerned from the writings of the prophets. Jesus is bringing about the time, as prophesied by Zechariah, when all nations will worship God in Jerusalem and when "there shall no longer be traders in the house of the Lord of hosts on that day" (Zech 14:21). Jesus quotes a passage from Isaiah: "My house shall be called a house of prayer for all the nations" (Isa 56:7). God desired the temple to be a sacred place where both Jews and Gentiles could worship God with reverence, but the commercialization of the Court of the Gentiles was preventing the temple precincts from being a place of prayer where Gentiles could also enter into God's presence. Jesus also alludes to the words of Jeremiah, "Has this house, which is called by my name, become a den of robbers in your sight?" (Jer 7:11). "A den of robbers" is where bandits take refuge and store what they have dishonestly obtained. Jeremiah was warning that God would destroy the temple because of those who try to hide their greed and injustices within its walls. Jesus offers this passage as a description of the corrupt practices of the temple leadership.

The prophetic action of Jesus causes the chief priests and scribes to fear him (verse 18). They seek a way to put him to death because he is a threat to their religious authority as well as a threat to their income and lifestyle. The withered fig tree and Jesus' action in the temple point to the judgment Jesus will bring on the temple. Meanwhile, he urges his disciples to deepen their faith and to trust in the power of prayer.

Reflection and discussion

• What is the relationship between the story of the fig tree and the cleansing of the temple?

• How do religious leaders sometimes hide their fruitlessness behind ceremonial foliage? In what ways might I do the same?

• How can I make my outward worship better express my inner faith?

Prayer

Lord of the temple, you desire the dwelling of your Father to be a house of prayer for all peoples. May the sacrifices I offer be true expressions of inner faith so that I may bear the fruit of holiness and justice in your kingdom.

**As Jesus was walking in the temple, the chief priests,
the scribes, and the elders came to him and said,
"By what authority are you doing these things?
Who gave you this authority to do them?"**
Mark 11:27–28

Controversy with the Religious Authorities in the Temple

MARK 11:27–12:27 *27Again they came to Jerusalem. As he was walking in the temple, the chief priests, the scribes, and the elders came to him 28and said, "By what authority are you doing these things? Who gave you this authority to do them?" 29Jesus said to them, "I will ask you one question; answer me, and I will tell you by what authority I do these things. 30Did the baptism of John come from heaven, or was it of human origin? Answer me." 31They argued with one another, "If we say, 'From heaven,' he will say, 'Why then did you not believe him?' 32But shall we say, 'Of human origin'?" —they were afraid of the crowd, for all regarded John as truly a prophet. 33So they answered Jesus, "We do not know." And Jesus said to them, "Neither will I tell you by what authority I am doing these things."*

12 *1Then he began to speak to them in parables. "A man planted a vineyard, put a fence around it, dug a pit for the wine press, and built a watchtower;*

then he leased it to tenants and went to another country. ²When the season came, he sent a slave to the tenants to collect from them his share of the produce of the vineyard. ³But they seized him, and beat him, and sent him away empty-handed. ⁴And again he sent another slave to them; this one they beat over the head and insulted. ⁵Then he sent another, and that one they killed. And so it was with many others; some they beat, and others they killed. ⁶He had still one other, a beloved son. Finally he sent him to them, saying, 'They will respect my son.' ⁷But those tenants said to one another, 'This is the heir; come, let us kill him, and the inheritance will be ours.' ⁸So they seized him, killed him, and threw him out of the vineyard. ⁹What then will the owner of the vineyard do? He will come and destroy the tenants and give the vineyard to others. ¹⁰Have you not read this scripture:

'The stone that the builders rejected
   has become the cornerstone;
¹¹this was the Lord's doing,
   and it is amazing in our eyes'?"

¹²When they realized that he had told this parable against them, they wanted to arrest him, but they feared the crowd. So they left him and went away.

¹³Then they sent to him some Pharisees and some Herodians to trap him in what he said. ¹⁴And they came and said to him, "Teacher, we know that you are sincere, and show deference to no one; for you do not regard people with partiality, but teach the way of God in accordance with truth. Is it lawful to pay taxes to the emperor, or not? ¹⁵Should we pay them, or should we not?" But knowing their hypocrisy, he said to them, "Why are you putting me to the test? Bring me a denarius and let me see it." ¹⁶And they brought one. Then he said to them, "Whose head is this, and whose title?" They answered, "The emperor's." ¹⁷Jesus said to them, "Give to the emperor the things that are the emperor's, and to God the things that are God's." And they were utterly amazed at him.

¹⁸Some Sadducees, who say there is no resurrection, came to him and asked him a question, saying, ¹⁹"Teacher, Moses wrote for us that 'if a man's brother dies, leaving a wife but no child, the man shall marry the widow and raise up children for his brother.' ²⁰There were seven brothers; the first married and, when he died, left no children; ²¹and the second married her and died, leaving no children; and the third likewise; ²²none of the seven left children. Last of all the woman herself died. ²³In the resurrection whose wife will she be? For the seven had married her."

²⁴*Jesus said to them, "Is not this the reason you are wrong, that you know neither the scriptures nor the power of God?* ²⁵*For when they rise from the dead, they neither marry nor are given in marriage, but are like angels in heaven.* ²⁶*And as for the dead being raised, have you not read in the book of Moses, in the story about the bush, how God said to him, 'I am the God of Abraham, the God of Isaac, and the God of Jacob'?* ²⁷*He is God not of the dead, but of the living; you are quite wrong."*

Knowing that confrontation is inevitable, Jesus walks back into the temple area where he enters into a series of conflicts with the religious authorities. In each case, the Jewish leaders come with questions designed to challenge and trap Jesus, but Jesus successfully escapes the snares of his opponents and uses the occasion to teach. He does not back away from conflict, but confronts people directly when something deserves criticism. But even when Jesus is harsh, his purpose is always to offer new insights and provoke deeper faith.

The central question of these episodes is asked by members of the Sanhedrin, the chief priests, scribes, and elders who make up the ruling body in Jerusalem: "By what authority are you doing these things?" What is the source of his authority to cast out demons, to forgive sins, to definitively interpret Scripture, to enter Jerusalem as its Messiah, and to judge the temple? Rather than answer their question directly, Jesus asks a counter question about the source of John's baptism. By their insincere and cowardly answer, "We do not know," the officials forfeit their right to expect an answer from Jesus as well as their claim to be the religious leaders of the nation (11:33).

In the parable of the vineyard, Jesus builds on the parable told by Isaiah in which Israel is the vineyard and God is the landlord (Isa 5:1–7). The tenants are the religious leaders of Israel who have been appointed by God to care for his people. The parable dramatizes the sad history of Israel as the prophets sent by God are rejected over and over again. The beloved son, the heir of God's vineyard, meets the same fate at the hands of Israel's leaders. Jesus is foretelling his passion: the tenants will seize the son, kill him, and drag him outside the vineyard. In response, Jesus says, God will "destroy the tenants and give the vineyard to others" (12:9). He is prophesying the destruction of the temple and its leadership and anticipating the new community of God's people open to both Jews and Gentiles. By quoting from Psalm 118, Jesus states that by rejecting him, they are rejecting the very cornerstone of God's new temple, the church (12:10).

The next question is posed to Jesus by the Pharisees and the Herodians. Designed to entrap Jesus in an inescapable dilemma, they ask, "Is it lawful to pay taxes to the emperor, or not?" (12:14). Depending on his answer, he would either destroy his popular support by supporting taxation or get arrested by the Roman authorities for stirring up a tax rebellion. But seeing their hypocrisy, Jesus uses the opportunity to teach. Not only does Jesus tell his listeners to "give to the emperor the things that are the emperor's," he also demands that they "give to God the things that are God's" (12:17). If the denarius belongs to the emperor because it was made with the emperor's image, then men and women owe to God their whole lives because they themselves were made in the image of God. Though Jesus' response does not resolve the conflicts that inevitably arise between one's duty to the state and one's responsibilities to God, this wise teaching of Jesus establishes a basic norm in the early church for living as members of the kingdom of God in the political domain of the state.

The question asked by the Sadducees is designed to show that belief in the resurrection is absurd, hoping to weaken Jesus' credibility as a teacher. The carefully crafted question derives from the command of Moses that if a man dies leaving a wife and no children, his brother should marry the wife and have children with her (Deut 25:5–6). The hypothetical case results in the marriage of seven brothers to the same woman without leaving any children. The question of the Sadducees, "In the resurrection whose wife will she be?" is designed to trap Jesus in an insoluble dilemma, disproving the resurrection (12:23). But using the question as an opportunity to teach, Jesus explains that God not only restores the dead to life but gives them a completely transformed existence. Human relationships in the resurrection will be so different that the situation posed by the Sadducees will not occur.

Reflection and discussion

• In what way does Jesus' parable of the vineyard answer the question of the religious leaders, "By what authority are you doing these things?"

• What are some conflicts of interest that can arise between a Christian's loyalty to civil government and loyalty to God?

• Why can I not know or understand what life will be like in the resurrection? What do I wish I knew?

Prayer

Good Teacher, you are the stone rejected by the builders that has become the cornerstone of God's temple. As you amazed those who tried to trap you and challenged your authority, help me to trust in your wisdom to guide my life.

"To love him with all the heart, and with all the understanding,
and with all the strength, and to love one's neighbor
as oneself—this is much more important than all whole
burnt offerings and sacrifices." Mark 12:33

The Debate in the Temple Concludes

MARK 12:28–44 ²⁸*One of the scribes came near and heard them disputing with one another, and seeing that he answered them well, he asked him, "Which commandment is the first of all?" ²⁹Jesus answered, "The first is, 'Hear, O Israel: the Lord our God, the Lord is one; ³⁰you shall love the Lord your God with all your heart, and with all your soul, and with all your mind, and with all your strength.' ³¹The second is this, 'You shall love your neighbor as yourself.' There is no other commandment greater than these." ³²Then the scribe said to him, "You are right, Teacher; you have truly said that 'he is one, and besides him there is no other'; ³³and 'to love him with all the heart, and with all the understanding, and with all the strength,' and 'to love one's neighbor as oneself,' —this is much more important than all whole burnt offerings and sacrifices." ³⁴When Jesus saw that he answered wisely, he said to him, "You are not far from the kingdom of God." After that no one dared to ask him any question.*

³⁵*While Jesus was teaching in the temple, he said, "How can the scribes say that the Messiah is the son of David? ³⁶David himself, by the Holy Spirit, declared,*

'The Lord said to my Lord,
 "Sit at my right hand,
       until I put your enemies under your feet."'
[37]David himself calls him Lord; so how can he be his son?" And the large crowd
was listening to him with delight.

[38]As he taught, he said, "Beware of the scribes, who like to walk around in
long robes, and to be greeted with respect in the marketplaces, [39]and to have the
best seats in the synagogues and places of honor at banquets! [40]They devour
widows' houses and for the sake of appearance say long prayers. They will
receive the greater condemnation."

[41]He sat down opposite the treasury, and watched the crowd putting money
into the treasury. Many rich people put in large sums. [42]A poor widow came and
put in two small copper coins, which are worth a penny. [43]Then he called his
disciples and said to them, "Truly I tell you, this poor widow has put in more
than all those who are contributing to the treasury. [44]For all of them have con-
tributed out of their abundance; but she out of her poverty has put in everything
she had, all she had to live on."

Unlike the previous questions asked by religious leaders, this inquiry
by the scribe is sincere and not intended to trap Jesus. The question
seeks to identify which commandment is the most fundamental on
which all the other commandments are based. Jesus' response begins by quoting the Shema, Israel's expression of faith in the one God to whom his people
must respond totally at every level of their being (verses 29–30; Deut 6:4–5).
This "first" commandment corresponds to the first table of the Decalogue and
deals with people's vertical relationship to God. Jesus then adds a "second"
commandment, which corresponds to the second table of the Decalogue and
deals with people's horizontal relationship with one another (verse 31; Lev
19:18). For Jesus, the second flows directly from the first; love of neighbor is
the expression of love for God. The "love" required in each commandment is
not just an abstract emotional feeling but an active obedience toward God and
acts of loving service for the wellbeing of others. When our hearts are set on
love for God and others, then the commandments become a joy and not a
burden. When love is our motivation, as the scribe affirms, then sacrifice and
religious practices become ways of expressing that love. Jesus commends the

understanding of the scribe and says that he is "not far from the kingdom of God." The scribe understands Jesus' teaching, he knows the way into the kingdom, and now all that he must do is follow the one in whose presence he stands.

When none of the religious leaders dare to ask Jesus any more questions, Jesus asks one of his own: "How can the scribes say that the Messiah is the son of David?" (verse 35). Jesus as the Messiah is indeed the Son of David, but that title is inadequate. As he quotes the first verse of Psalm 110, Jesus first emphasizes the psalm's authority by noting that David, in composing the psalm, was inspired by the Holy Spirit. Second, he shows that in speaking of the Messiah, David is speaking of his Lord: "The Lord (God) said to my Lord (the Messiah), 'Sit at my right hand.'" Jesus is not denying that he is the messianic descendant of David, but he is demonstrating that he is much more. He is indeed David's Lord, the Son of God. At God's right hand, he will rule over not only the kingdom of David but also the whole of God's creation.

Because Jesus has just commended a sincere scribe seeking God's kingdom, his stern words about the practices of Jerusalem's scribes are not meant to denounce them all. Rather, Jesus admonishes religious leaders who demonstrate arrogance, practice false piety, and abuse religion for personal gain. Most importantly, Jesus is offering negative examples for the future leaders of his church to avoid. He is not condemning respectful titles, distinctive attire, and places of honor for leaders in the church. Rather, he firmly warns of the dangers of such marks of esteem because it is so easy to begin seeking and encouraging them, considering oneself entitled to them, and even using them to take advantage of others.

Mark closes this section of his gospel with the image of the poor widow, as Jesus calls his disciples to notice her deed. In offering her two small coins she gives "everything" she has, literally, her whole life (verse 44). Although the copper coin was the smallest coin in circulation, her gift is immeasurable because she has given her all. Her complete self-giving foreshadows the self-sacrifice that Jesus is about to make—the offering of his very life without reservation. The woman, in contrast to the self-seeking scribes, forms a positive model for Jesus' present and future disciples to imitate.

Reflection and discussion

• What would love of God be without love of neighbor? What would love of neighbor be without love of God? Why does Jesus link these two commandments inseparably?

• Why did Jesus point out both the scribes and the poor widow to his disciples? What does he want the leaders of his church to understand from their example?

• How can I avoid hypocritical religious practice? How can I make my discipleship more generous and uncalculating?

Prayer

Son of David and Son of God, you teach us that love of God and love of neighbor are more important than all the sacrifices and offerings in the temple. Teach me to open my heart to you and to give of myself generously and trustingly.

"For nation will rise against nation, and kingdom against kingdom; there will be earthquakes in various places; there will be famines. This is but the beginning of the birthpangs." Mark 13:8

Destruction of the Temple and Persecutions to Come

MARK 13:1–23 ¹*As he came out of the temple, one of his disciples said to him, "Look, Teacher, what large stones and what large buildings!" ²Then Jesus asked him, "Do you see these great buildings? Not one stone will be left here upon another; all will be thrown down."*

³*When he was sitting on the Mount of Olives opposite the temple, Peter, James, John, and Andrew asked him privately, ⁴"Tell us, when will this be, and what will be the sign that all these things are about to be accomplished?" ⁵Then Jesus began to say to them, "Beware that no one leads you astray. ⁶Many will come in my name and say, 'I am he!' and they will lead many astray. ⁷When you hear of wars and rumors of wars, do not be alarmed; this must take place, but the end is still to come. ⁸For nation will rise against nation, and kingdom against kingdom; there will be earthquakes in various places; there will be famines. This is but the beginning of the birthpangs.*

⁹*"As for yourselves, beware; for they will hand you over to councils; and you will be beaten in synagogues; and you will stand before governors and kings*

because of me, as a testimony to them. ¹⁰*And the good news must first be pro-claimed to all nations.* ¹¹*When they bring you to trial and hand you over, do not worry beforehand about what you are to say; but say whatever is given you at that time, for it is not you who speak, but the Holy Spirit.* ¹²*Brother will betray brother to death, and a father his child, and children will rise against parents and have them put to death;* ¹³*and you will be hated by all because of my name. But the one who endures to the end will be saved.*

¹⁴*"But when you see the desolating sacrilege set up where it ought not to be (let the reader understand), then those in Judea must flee to the mountains;* ¹⁵*the one on the housetop must not go down or enter the house to take anything away;* ¹⁶*the one in the field must not turn back to get a coat.* ¹⁷*Woe to those who are pregnant and to those who are nursing infants in those days!* ¹⁸*Pray that it may not be in winter.* ¹⁹*For in those days there will be suffering, such as has not been from the beginning of the creation that God created until now, no, and never will be.* ²⁰*And if the Lord had not cut short those days, no one would be saved; but for the sake of the elect, whom he chose, he has cut short those days.* ²¹*And if anyone says to you at that time, 'Look! Here is the Messiah!' or 'Look! There he is!' —do not believe it.* ²²*False messiahs and false prophets will appear and pro-duce signs and omens, to lead astray, if possible, the elect.* ²³*But be alert; I have already told you everything.*

A s Jesus leaves the temple for the last time, one of his disciples com-ments on the magnificence of its construction. The Jerusalem temple rested on a foundation of massive limestone, and its façade was white marble adorned with dazzling gold. Naturally the disciples of Jesus were proud of Israel's national shrine, which represented the presence of God with his people, their sacrificial worship, and their hopes for the future. Nothing seemed more permanent and indestructible than the temple. Yet, Jesus replies that "not one stone will be left here upon another," prophesying its complete destruction. Like the temple of Solomon, destroyed in 587 B.C. as divine judg-ment upon its corrupt leadership, this second temple would be destroyed in A.D. 70 by the Roman armies.

This longest of all Jesus' teachings takes place on the Mount of Olives while he and his closest disciples gaze upon the city and its temple. In response to their question concerning the time and the signs of this occurrence, Jesus offers a series of tribulations: first, deceivers will come claiming to be the Messiah and will lead many astray; second, there will be wars and rumors of wars; and third, there will be earthquakes and famines. Such occurrences were common throughout the Roman empire of the time. Jesus assures his disciples that these trials are only "the beginnings of the birth pangs" (verse 8). This bittersweet image suggests that, like the pains of a woman in labor, the tribulations will come in successive waves with increasing distress, but will lead to a joy and new life that far outshine the pain.

As Jesus continues his discourse, he prepares his disciples for a difficult time of persecution. Their sufferings are described in ways that parallel the passion of Jesus. Like him, they will be handed over and brought to trial before religious authorities in the form of councils and synagogues as well as civil authorities in the form of governors and kings (verse 9). Yet, the history of the early church demonstrates that these persecutions are the very means by which disciples will bear witness to Jesus and spread the message of the gospel throughout the world. The purpose of the teaching is to exhort disciples of Jesus and the church of Mark to be faithful during deceptions, trials, and suffering. Through these birth pangs, the good news will be proclaimed to all the nations, and those who persevere in faith will be saved (verse 13).

Although deceivers, wars, earthquakes, famines, and persecutions warn of the coming end, the surest signal will be "the desolating sacrilege" (verse 14). Using biblical imagery of God's judgment from the prophets, Jesus foretells the calamities that will accompany the destruction of the temple. The great sacrilege refers to the Roman army occupying the temple, the worst possible desecration for a Jew. Since utter destruction is inevitable, all must flee from Jerusalem without delay to escape the slaughter. The disaster will be experienced by the wicked and the innocent alike, and as happens so often in wars and tragedies, women and children will bear the brunt of the suffering. This will signal the most devastating period of tribulation God's people have ever endured.

Yet God's mercy shines in the midst of this dark forecast. The future is in God's hands. "For the sake of the elect," those chosen by God to be members of his church, God has shortened the days of tribulation (verse 20). Jesus has urged his followers to "be alert" and has prepared them for what lies ahead. Despite the destruction of the temple and the end of the old covenant with its sacrificial worship, God has laid a new cornerstone in Jesus.

Reflection and discussion

• Why was the destruction of the temple such a world-shattering event for the Jewish people?

• Although Jesus does not offer reasons for the occurrence of natural disasters, wars, and famines, he does characterize the human suffering they cause as "birth pangs." How is this image both realistic and hopeful?

• Why does Jesus describe the persecutions of his disciples in ways that parallel his own passion?

Prayer

Lord Jesus, you help me understand that the trials I endure are necessary to experience the new life you desire for me. Help me to persevere in my afflictions and to be alert and ready for the completion of your plan.

"But about that day or hour no one knows, neither the angels in heaven, nor the Son, but only the Father. Beware, keep alert; for you do not know when the time will come." Mark 13:32–33

The Need for Watchfulness

MARK 13:24–37

²⁴"But in those days, after that suffering,
the sun will be darkened,
    and the moon will not give its light,
²⁵and the stars will be falling from heaven,
    and the powers in the heavens will be shaken.
²⁶Then they will see 'the Son of Man coming in clouds' with great power and glory. ²⁷Then he will send out the angels, and gather his elect from the four winds, from the ends of the earth to the ends of heaven.

²⁸"From the fig tree learn its lesson: as soon as its branch becomes tender and puts forth its leaves, you know that summer is near. ²⁹So also, when you see these things taking place, you know that he is near, at the very gates. ³⁰Truly I tell you, this generation will not pass away until all these things have taken place. ³¹Heaven and earth will pass away, but my words will not pass away.

³²"But about that day or hour no one knows, neither the angels in heaven, nor the Son, but only the Father. ³³Beware, keep alert; for you do not know when the time will come. ³⁴It is like a man going on a journey, when he leaves home and

puts his slaves in charge, each with his work, and commands the doorkeeper to be on the watch. [35]Therefore, keep awake—for you do not know when the master of the house will come, in the evening, or at midnight, or at cockcrow, or at dawn, [36]or else he may find you asleep when he comes suddenly. [37]And what I say to you I say to all: Keep awake."

I
n his final discourse, Jesus refers to different events, often at the same time. He speaks of his own suffering and death, the persecution of his followers, the coming destruction of the temple, and also the end of the world. He overlays close and distant events to reveal their connection with one another. The passion of Jesus is the beginning of the end of history. His anguish and death point to the future suffering and martyrdom of those who follow him, and the end of the temple points to the end of the world. These events are all shown to be linked together through the use of prophetic language.

The cosmic language of the darkened sun and moon along with falling stars refers to apocalyptic symbols used in Isaiah, Ezekiel, Joel, and Amos to anticipate the day of God's judgment upon ancient cities and empires (verses 24–25). Ultimately, this cosmic upheaval points to the end of the world, but the gospel hints at other levels of meaning. Mark shows that the death of Jesus on the cross was the beginning of this time of God's judgment as the sun darkened at midday (15:33). Likewise, the language refers to the fall of Jerusalem and the destruction of the temple. Israel's temple was the center of the universe and the meeting point between heaven and earth. Its destruction by the invading Roman armies was a catastrophe of cosmic proportions.

These devastating events are the necessary prelude to God's victory, the birth pangs that precede the fullness of life. The Son of Man is the title Jesus has used most often of himself, especially in predicting his passion, death, and resurrection. The image of the Son of Man coming into God's presence "in clouds with great power and glory" evokes the prophecy of Daniel and is used by Jesus to speak of himself (verse 26; Dan 7:13–14). He again overlays close and distant events to reveal their connections. On one level, the image refers to Jesus in his risen glory, ascending to the Father and seated at his right hand. Ultimately, it speaks of his coming at the end of time, when the powers of evil are destroyed, suffering ended, and the Son of God will be seen by all in the fullness of his power and glory. He will then gather his "elect," those who have remained faithful throughout the time of distress, from all parts of the world.

Just as surely as the sprouting leaves of the fig tree indicate that summer is near, the cataclysmic events about which Jesus has spoken indicate that the former age is drawing to a close and the new age of God's kingdom is upon the world. Jesus' assurance that "this generation will not pass away until all these things have taken place" indicates that his passion, death, and resurrection, as well as the destruction of the temple and the age of the church, are events that will happen during the lifetime of the present generation (verse 30). The final events, however, the fullness of the kingdom and the end of time—"about that day or hour no one knows" (verse 32).

The primary lesson of this final discourse comes in its continual refrain: "Beware" (verses 5, 9, 33), "Be alert" (verses 23, 33), "Keep awake" (verses 35, 37). Since it is impossible to know when the day of the Lord's coming might be, the call to all disciples of Jesus, in the first century or the twenty-first century, is to live with an attitude of vigilance, alertness, and watchfulness so as not to be caught unprepared. We should live as if Christ might return at any moment and ask us to account for what we have done with our lives. But the discourse is not only a warning but also a joyous anticipation of the coming of the Lord, the blessed hope for which the whole church longs and prays.

Reflection and discussion

• What is the good news in this discourse about suffering and persecution in the Christian life?

• How does Jesus express the foolishness of trying to predict the time of the end? What does he recommend we do instead?

• How might my life be different if I truly lived with watchfulness, expectancy, and vigilance?

• What is most hopeful to me about this final discourse of Jesus?

Prayer

Lord of glory, may I keep my heart ready to meet you. Since I may come face to face with you any day, either through my own death or through your glorious return, keep me watchful, awake, and ready.

SUGGESTIONS FOR FACILITATORS, GROUP SESSION 4

1. Welcome group members and ask if anyone has any questions, announcements, or requests.

2. You may want to pray this prayer as a group:

God of all people, your Son arrived in Jerusalem and humbly entered the city and its temple. As Son of David, he was welcomed with shouts of Hosanna. As Lord of the temple, he cleansed your dwelling to make it a house of prayer for all the nations. As the stone rejected by the builders, he will become the Cornerstone of the new temple. As the Lord, he will sit at the right hand of God. As Master of the house, he will return at a time we do not expect. As Son of Man, he will come with power and glory. Keep me watchful and ready, confident that your words will not pass away.

3. Ask one or more of the following questions:
   - What is the most difficult part of this study for you?
   - What insights stand out to you from the lessons this week?

4. Discuss lessons 13 through 18. Choose one or more of the questions for reflection and discussion from each lesson to discuss as a group. You may want to ask group members which question was most challenging or helpful to them as you review each lesson.

5. Keep the discussion moving, but allow time for the questions that provoke the most discussion. Encourage the group members to use "I" language in their responses.

6. After talking over each lesson, instruct group members to complete lessons 19 through 24 on their own during the six days before the next group meeting. They should write out their own answers to the questions as preparation for next week's session.

7. Ask the group what encouragement they need for the coming week. Ask the members to pray for the needs of one another during the week.

8. Conclude by praying aloud together the prayer at the end of one of the lessons discussed. You may choose to conclude the prayer by asking members to pray aloud any requests they may have.

"Truly I tell you, wherever the good news is proclaimed in the whole world, what she has done will be told in remembrance of her." Mark 14:9

Devotion and Treachery

MARK 14:1–11   ¹*It was two days before the Passover and the festival of Unleavened Bread. The chief priests and the scribes were looking for a way to arrest Jesus by stealth and kill him; ²for they said, "Not during the festival, or there may be a riot among the people."*

³*While he was at Bethany in the house of Simon the leper, as he sat at the table, a woman came with an alabaster jar of very costly ointment of nard, and she broke open the jar and poured the ointment on his head. ⁴But some were there who said to one another in anger, "Why was the ointment wasted in this way? ⁵For this ointment could have been sold for more than three hundred denarii, and the money given to the poor." And they scolded her. ⁶But Jesus said, "Let her alone; why do you trouble her? She has performed a good service for me. ⁷For you always have the poor with you, and you can show kindness to them whenever you wish; but you will not always have me. ⁸She has done what she could; she has anointed my body beforehand for its burial. ⁹Truly I tell you, wherever the good news is proclaimed in the whole world, what she has done will be told in remembrance of her."*

¹⁰*Then Judas Iscariot, who was one of the twelve, went to the chief priests in order to betray him to them. ¹¹When they heard it, they were greatly pleased, and promised to give him money. So he began to look for an opportunity to betray him.*

T he passion account begins as Mark notes the upcoming Passover festival, the annual commemoration of the redemption of the Israelites
from their slavery in Egypt. During this festival, the population of
Jerusalem swells with pilgrims from throughout the world while hopes of
deliverance from the bondage of the Romans deepen. The religious leaders
are seeking a way to seize Jesus "by stealth" because they fear his popularity
with the people and want to avoid an uprising during the days of the festival.

Into this dark scene of treachery, Mark shines the gospel light on the
woman at Bethany. Like the poor widow at the temple, this woman offers the
disciples of Jesus a model of loving generosity. Her extravagant love foreshadows the unreserved giving that Jesus will demonstrate on the cross. Rather
than opening the jar and measuring out an appropriate amount, the woman
breaks the neck of the alabaster jar and lavishly pours the entire amount on
the head of Jesus. She breaks and pours out her greatest treasure on Jesus, as
he will break and pour out his life for all people.

Nard oil was an expensive ointment from the roots of a rare Indian plant.
The monetary worth of the oil, calculated at "more than three hundred denarii,"
was about a year's wages for an ordinary worker (verse 5). Those who observe
the scene protest that surely this oil could have been put to more practical use
in the form of alms for the poor. Yet, Jesus interrupts their scolding and praises
her action. His additional comment, "For you always have the poor with you,
and you can show kindness to them whenever you wish," is not a justification
for letting people live in poverty. Rather, his words allude to the Torah's directive
to care for the needy: "Since there will never cease to be some in need in the
earth, I therefore command you, 'Open your hand to the poor and needy neighbor in your land'" (Deut 15:11). Though God's people must always care for the
needy, their opportunity to care for Jesus is drawing to a close.

Jesus interprets the woman's deed as an anointing of his body beforehand
for burial (verse 8). Corpses were customarily anointed with perfumed oil
before being placed in the tomb, and the woman offers the only anointing
Jesus will receive. After his death, the body of Jesus will be placed in the tomb
without the usual anointing because of the approach of the Sabbath. Through
this anointing, the woman is giving what she could to Jesus, who will give his
life for her.

In contrast to the woman who responds to Jesus with sacrificial generosity,
Judas Iscariot selfishly betrays Jesus for money. The betrayal is particularly

horrible since Judas is one of the Twelve, a close and trusted companion of Jesus (verse 10). While the woman sacrifices her money for her faith, Judas sacrifices his faith for money. He informs the religious leaders how Jesus could be seized by stealth while away from his popular support base. Judas knew that Jesus would be spending the night of Passover on the Mount of Olives, so he arranged how they could seize him there. Although Judas is part of the cosmic drama of Jesus' death, the narrative emphasizes his freedom in making his tragic choice.

Reflection and discussion

• Why does Mark insert the story about the woman at Bethany between the plotting of the religious leaders and the betrayal of Judas?

• How could Judas have betrayed Jesus after being so close to him?

• What might be something selfless and extravagant that I could do for Jesus in response to his total self-giving for me?

Prayer

Lord Jesus, you give me the example of the selfless woman as an example of love for you. Open my heart to love you more and to express my love with generous deeds.

"This is my blood of the covenant, which is poured out for many. Truly I tell you, I will never again drink of the fruit of the vine until that day when I drink it new in the kingdom of God." Mark 14:24–25

The Last Supper with His Disciples

MARK 14:12–31 ¹²*On the first day of Unleavened Bread, when the Passover lamb is sacrificed, his disciples said to him, "Where do you want us to go and make the preparations for you to eat the Passover?" ¹³So he sent two of his disciples, saying to them, "Go into the city, and a man carrying a jar of water will meet you; follow him, ¹⁴and wherever he enters, say to the owner of the house, 'The Teacher asks, Where is my guest room where I may eat the Passover with my disciples?' ¹⁵He will show you a large room upstairs, furnished and ready. Make preparations for us there." ¹⁶So the disciples set out and went to the city, and found everything as he had told them; and they prepared the Passover meal.*

¹⁷*When it was evening, he came with the twelve. ¹⁸And when they had taken their places and were eating, Jesus said, "Truly I tell you, one of you will betray me, one who is eating with me." ¹⁹They began to be distressed and to say to him one after another, "Surely, not I?" ²⁰He said to them, "It is one of the twelve, one who is dipping bread into the bowl with me. ²¹For the Son of Man goes as it is written of him, but woe to that one by whom the Son of Man is betrayed! It would have been better for that one not to have been born."*

²²*While they were eating, he took a loaf of bread, and after blessing it he*

broke it, gave it to them, and said, "Take; this is my body." ²³*Then he took a cup, and after giving thanks he gave it to them, and all of them drank from it.* ²⁴*He said to them, "This is my blood of the covenant, which is poured out for many.* ²⁵*Truly I tell you, I will never again drink of the fruit of the vine until that day when I drink it new in the kingdom of God."*

²⁶*When they had sung the hymn, they went out to the Mount of Olives.* ²⁷*And Jesus said to them, "You will all become deserters; for it is written,*

> *'I will strike the shepherd,*
> *and the sheep will be scattered.'*

²⁸*But after I am raised up, I will go before you to Galilee."* ²⁹*Peter said to him, "Even though all become deserters, I will not."* ³⁰*Jesus said to him, "Truly I tell you, this day, this very night, before the cock crows twice, you will deny me three times."* ³¹*But he said vehemently, "Even though I must die with you, I will not deny you." And all of them said the same.*

After sunset, as Passover began, Jewish families would gather in Jerusalem to remember the saving events that made them God's people and rededicate themselves to their covenant with God. In the Passover meal, they also looked forward to the future and longed for the redemption that God had continually promised them through the prophets. This Passover meal would be the last meal Jesus would share with his disciples. Having made arrangements in advance to have a large upstairs room furnished and ready for the meal, Jesus sends two of his disciples to secure the room and prepare for the meal. The discreet signals are designed to elude the religious leaders who were on the lookout for an opportunity to arrest Jesus.

Although sharing a meal is the greatest expression of communion among friends in the Jewish culture, as this last supper begins, Jesus reveals a terrible breach of loyalty: "One of you will betray me" (verse 18). Jesus emphasizes the heinous nature of the betrayal with this progression: "one of you," "one who is eating with me," "one of the twelve," "one who is dipping bread into the bowl with me." The treachery seems to particularly echo a psalm of lament: "Even my bosom friend in whom I trusted, who ate of my bread, has lifted the heel against me" (Ps 41:9).

The reader is drawn into the shocked response of the disciples. One by one they ask Jesus, "Surely, not I?" (verse 19). The reader is called to repeat the question in turn. Because Jesus does not yet identify who it is who will betray him, each disciple must humbly recognize the evil of which he is capable, and every reader of the gospel must realize that he or she could potentially prove unfaithful in a similar way.

The actions of Jesus with the bread, as he takes, blesses, breaks, and gives it to his disciples, are the same gestures he performed at the two accounts in which he fed both Jews and Gentiles in abundance. In the disciples' failure to understand the meaning of the loaves, Mark showed their failure to understand Jesus and the meaning of his mission (6:52; 8:17–21). At this meal of the new Passover, Jesus goes further and identifies the loaf with his body, his very self. As Jesus is about to be handed over, broken, and put to death, this eucharistic action expresses Jesus' sacrificial gift of himself for others. As Jesus broke the bread for the crowds, expressing his mission as the Messiah, so his action at the meal expresses the final act of that mission as he gives his very self.

The cup refers to the sacrificial death of Jesus in other passages of the gospel, a death which the disciples are invited to share (10:38–39; 14:36). In his final meal before death, Jesus identifies the cup of wine with his blood, the "blood of the covenant, which is poured out for many" (verse 24). "For many" is an idiom that means "for the great masses of the people," both Jews and Gentiles. As the flesh of a lamb and the sprinkling of its blood marked God's covenant with Israel, now the new sacrificial meal of Jesus' body and blood seals the new covenant to be accomplished on the cross.

The central element of the Passover meal, the sacrificed lamb whose blood saved the Israelites from death, is not mentioned in this account. But Jesus' words and gestures reveal that he himself is the Lamb, whose blood will save the great masses from eternal death. Just as the Passover sacrifice was not complete without eating the lamb, Jesus' sacrifice is complete only when his disciples consume his body and blood.

After the meal, the scene again becomes dark and foreboding as Jesus and his disciples cross the valley to the Mount of Olives. Before the meal, Jesus had prophesied the failure of one disciple; now he prophesies the failure of all: "You will all become deserters" (verse 27). Again, the gospel draws in the reader to Jesus' inclusive prediction of broken discipleship. All will scatter in disillusionment and fear. But Jesus does not end his prophecy with abandonment. He announces his resurrection and the restoration of the disciples in Galilee.

Peter's protest is reminiscent of his response to Jesus' first passion prediction (8:32–33). With his characteristic brashness, Peter said, "Even though all become deserters, I will not" (verse 29). Peter's loyalty and love for Jesus are not yet matched by sober self-knowledge and humility. Jesus responds to Peter's presumptuousness by stating that Peter would deny him three times that very night. Once more Peter rebukes Jesus with a vehement protest, and the other disciples join in the rebuttal (verse 31). The shallow loyalty of the disciples, as they refuse to accept Jesus' words about the cross, forms a strong contrast to the absolute devotion of Jesus who gives himself completely for them.

Reflection and discussion

• What are the various meanings of the Eucharist as stressed in Mark's account?

• In what sense is celebrating Eucharist the renewal of the covenant established on the cross?

• Why was Peter so overconfident in his discipleship? Why was he unprepared for the crisis of Jesus' arrest?

Prayer

Eucharistic Lord, disciples in every age have shared in the sacrificial meal that you instituted at Passover. Guide me to participate in the renewal of your sacrifice on the cross, to celebrate your real presence, and to deepen the new covenant which inspires me to work for the coming of God's kingdom.

"Abba, Father, for you all things are possible; remove this cup from me; yet, not what I want, but what you want." Mark 14:36

Jesus Prays in Gethsemane

MARK 14:32–42 *32They went to a place called Gethsemane; and he said to his disciples, "Sit here while I pray." 33He took with him Peter and James and John, and began to be distressed and agitated. 34And he said to them, "I am deeply grieved, even to death; remain here, and keep awake." 35And going a little farther, he threw himself on the ground and prayed that, if it were possible, the hour might pass from him. 36He said, "Abba, Father, for you all things are possible; remove this cup from me; yet, not what I want, but what you want." 37He came and found them sleeping; and he said to Peter, "Simon, are you asleep? Could you not keep awake one hour? 38Keep awake and pray that you may not come into the time of trial; the spirit indeed is willing, but the flesh is weak." 39And again he went away and prayed, saying the same words. 40And once more he came and found them sleeping, for their eyes were very heavy; and they did not know what to say to him. 41He came a third time and said to them, "Are you still sleeping and taking your rest? Enough! The hour has come; the Son of Man is betrayed into the hands of sinners. 42Get up, let us be going. See, my betrayer is at hand."*

After the meal of the new Passover, the journey of Jesus and his disciples concludes at a place called Gethsemane. In this grove of olive trees on the slope of the Mount of Olives, we witness the anguished prayer of Jesus before he is arrested and the repeated failure of his closest disciples to watch with him.

Jesus brings Peter, James, and John with him to pray. These are the same disciples who were present at the transfiguration of Jesus. In both scenes Jesus takes the three disciples aside from the others to reveal the depth of his mission. Just as they witnessed Jesus in glory, they now see him in anguish and weakness as he faces death. If they are to truly know and follow Jesus, they must understand his suffering as well as his glory. These chosen disciples also heard his discourse on the Mount of Olives about the coming tribulation. Then Jesus warned them to watch and pray because no one knows the day or the hour when the terrible trial will take place. If they are to be his disciples, they must always live in watchful expectation.

In this hour of deep pain, Jesus had to make the most important decision of his life. Mark vividly describes his anguish and fear. He falls to the ground and cries out to his Father like a child in need. The Aramaic word "Abba" is preserved here because this was the habitual address of Jesus to God. At his baptism and transfiguration, Jesus was proclaimed as God's beloved Son. Now this deep and intimate union between the Father and the Son is acclaimed by Jesus as he prays.

Although Jesus has been shown throughout the gospel as destined to lay down his life, to "drink the cup," now as the time approaches, Jesus pours out his heart in a profound and emotional lament and prays that the cup be taken away. What Jesus experiences at Gethsemane is not only the dread of suffering but the full weight of human sin and its consequent alienation from God. He enters into the depths of the human condition to transform it from within. Despite his human fears and anguish, the bedrock of Jesus' lament is the Father's will: "Not what I want, but what you want" (verse 36). The Son of Man will drink the cup and thereby bring about the most perfect act of love conceivable from a human heart.

The fervent prayer of Jesus strongly contrasts with the disciples' behavior. Before entering into prayer, Jesus warns them to "keep awake." These words echo the final words of his last discourse: "What I say to you I say to all: Keep awake" (13:37). Yet, after each prayer of Jesus the results are the same: the disciples fall asleep instead of keeping watch. Three times Jesus returns from prayer and finds them sleeping. The triple failure of the disciples parallels the three times that Peter will deny Jesus before the night is over.

Jesus urges these three disciples along with all future disciples, "Keep awake and pray that you may not come into the time of trial" (verse 38). This "time of trial" is the same word used for the tempting of Jesus by Satan at the beginning of the gospel (1:13). This testing will continue in the lives of Jesus' disciples as they struggle with the power of evil in the world. Jesus recognizes the conflicting dimensions within each person: "the spirit," which is responsive to God's will, and "the flesh," which is egotistical and opposed to God's will. After Jesus finds his disciples sleeping for a third time, he announces that the hour has come and he is about to be betrayed. Through his prayer Jesus is now prepared for his arrest and passion. However, the disciples who failed to keep awake in vigilant prayer will soon flee in fear.

Reflection and discussion

• If I imagine I am with Jesus in Gethsemane, what emotions do I feel? What does this imaginative experience add to my understanding of this scene?

• Why would Jesus ask his Father to spare him from what he knew was his Father's will for him? Can I accept that Jesus experienced struggles similar to my own?

Prayer

Lord Jesus, you felt anguish and abandonment in the presence of your Father and your three closest disciples. Give me the grace to learn from your obedience to the Father and to entrust my life to him.

Now the betrayer had given them a sign, saying, "The one I will kiss
is the man; arrest him and lead him away under guard." Mark 14:44

Jesus Is Arrested
While the Disciples Flee

MARK 14:43–52 *⁴³Immediately, while he was still speaking, Judas, one of
the twelve, arrived; and with him there was a crowd with swords and clubs, from
the chief priests, the scribes, and the elders. ⁴⁴Now the betrayer had given them
a sign, saying, "The one I will kiss is the man; arrest him and lead him away
under guard." ⁴⁵So when he came, he went up to him at once and said, "Rabbi!"
and kissed him. ⁴⁶Then they laid hands on him and arrested him. ⁴⁷But one of
those who stood near drew his sword and struck the slave of the high priest, cut-
ting off his ear. ⁴⁸Then Jesus said to them, "Have you come out with swords and
clubs to arrest me as though I were a bandit? ⁴⁹Day after day I was with you in
the temple teaching, and you did not arrest me. But let the scriptures be fulfilled."
⁵⁰All of them deserted him and fled.*

*⁵¹A certain young man was following him, wearing nothing but a linen cloth.
They caught hold of him, ⁵²but he left the linen cloth and ran off naked.*

Again, Judas in introduced as "one of the twelve," emphasizing the
treacherous nature of his betrayal. He arrives in Gethsemane with a
crowd sent from the religious leaders of Jerusalem to arrest Jesus.

The temple police and others sent by the religious officials are armed with swords and clubs, prepared for a violent confrontation. That they represent the temple officials is evident from Jesus' words to them: "Day after day I was with you in the temple teaching, and you did not arrest me." The chief priest, scribes, and elders had been seeking to arrest Jesus since their confrontation with him in the temple, but they feared the crowds who supported Jesus. Now, through the betrayal of Judas, they have found a way to arrest him by stealth in the cover of darkness. Jesus' words reveal their cowardice in coming to seize Jesus at night rather than in the light of day.

Even though the Passover setting means that the moon was full, in the darkness of the olive grove it would have been difficult to distinguish Jesus from the thousands of other pilgrims camping on the hills surrounding Jerusalem. The prearranged signal is the kiss of Judas. A kiss on the cheeks was a frequent form of greeting for a rabbi and his follower. Judas' kiss and his respectful greeting emphasize the despicable nature of his betrayal of Jesus. Now that Jesus has been identified, he is immediately seized and arrested.

Jesus' prediction that all of his disciples would become deserters is here fulfilled. The complete abandonment of Jesus by his closest followers is starkly described: "All of them deserted him and fled" (verse 50). This total flight of the disciples is further dramatized by a brief scene that is only present in Mark's account of the passion. A young man following Jesus leaves even his clothing to escape from the scene (verses 51–52). Fleeing naked is a sign of shame, demonstrating that the young man chooses shame over faithfulness. This anonymous follower emphasizes the total desertion of Jesus by his followers, and challenges the readers of Mark's gospel to consider their own commitment to remain with Jesus in crisis.

Throughout his gospel, Mark never hesitates to show us the weakness of the disciples. They continually misunderstand Jesus and argue among themselves. Here, during the climactic time of Jesus' life, Mark shows them at their worst. They all disown Jesus when he needs them the most. Judas betrays him with a kiss, Peter will deny him, and his closest disciples cannot even stay awake with Jesus in his most desperate hour. As Jesus is arrested, all his disciples flee and are not seen again during his passion. Even the young man, who could represent any one of us, is in such a haste to flee that he leaves his clothes behind. Jesus is totally deserted and left to face his trials alone.

Reflection and discussion

• Why did Mark choose to emphasize the faults and failings of the disciples so emphatically throughout the gospel?

• When have I felt intimidated or afraid to follow Jesus? What do I need to be a more faithful disciple?

• Some commentators have suggested that the young man at the end of this scene is Mark himself. If this is so, what does this say to me about Mark and his gospel?

Prayer

Suffering Lord, at your darkest hour you were betrayed and abandoned by your friends. Help me recognize my own weaknesses and my capacity to deny, betray, and abandon you. Strengthen me with your grace, and prepare me for the most difficult hour.

The high priest asked him, "Are you the Messiah,
the Son of the Blessed One?" Jesus said, "I am." Mark 14:61–62

Jesus Is Accused
before the Sanhedrin

MARK 14:53–65 ⁵³*They took Jesus to the high priest; and all the chief priests, the elders, and the scribes were assembled.* ⁵⁴*Peter had followed him at a distance, right into the courtyard of the high priest; and he was sitting with the guards, warming himself at the fire.* ⁵⁵*Now the chief priests and the whole council were looking for testimony against Jesus to put him to death; but they found none.* ⁵⁶*For many gave false testimony against him, and their testimony did not agree.* ⁵⁷*Some stood up and gave false testimony against him, saying,* ⁵⁸*"We heard him say, 'I will destroy this temple that is made with hands, and in three days I will build another, not made with hands.'"* ⁵⁹*But even on this point their testimony did not agree.* ⁶⁰*Then the high priest stood up before them and asked Jesus, "Have you no answer? What is it that they testify against you?"* ⁶¹*But he was silent and did not answer. Again the high priest asked him, "Are you the Messiah, the Son of the Blessed One?"* ⁶²*Jesus said, "I am; and*

'you will see the Son of Man
seated at the right hand of the Power,'
and 'coming with the clouds of heaven.'"

⁶³*Then the high priest tore his clothes and said, "Why do we still need witnesses?* ⁶⁴*You have heard his blasphemy! What is your decision?" All of them con-*

demned him as deserving death. ⁶⁵*Some began to spit on him, to blindfold him, and to strike him, saying to him, "Prophesy!" The guards also took him over and beat him.*

Mark sets the trial of Jesus in between the account of Peter's denial. While Peter is in the courtyard, fearful and warming himself by the fire, Jesus is courageously confessing his identity before the Sanhedrin, the highest religious authority in the land. The trial is held at night because the leaders fear Jesus' popularity with the Jewish people and desire to deal with him quickly before the people could react.

Although the charge against Jesus is not yet determined, the decision to put Jesus to death has already been made (verse 55). The officials are seeking testimony from witnesses in order to support their decision. But the testimony does not permit a guilty verdict because the witnesses do not agree with one another. In fact, the only testimony documented in Mark's account is described as false.

The testimony of the witnesses focuses on Jesus' relationship with the temple. After entering Jerusalem, Jesus had cleansed the temple courts and critiqued the temple worship. In his final discourse on the Mount of Olives he told his closest disciples that the temple would be destroyed, and he related its destruction to the death of the Messiah. The gospel has shown how each of Jesus' statements about the temple leads to the plot on his life by the temple officials. Yet, the central charge against Jesus is described as false: "We heard him say, 'I will destroy this temple that is made with hands, and in three days I will build another, not made with hands'" (verse 58). Jesus neither admits nor denies their accusation, and Mark allows it to remain ambiguous. On the one hand, the statement misrepresents the ministry of Jesus. He is not a militant who intends to destroy the physical structure of the temple, but rather he is the suffering Messiah who will himself be destroyed. On the other hand, the saving ministry and death of Jesus will destroy the need and efficacy of the temple, and establish a new, spiritual temple of which he himself is the cornerstone.

While the destruction of the temple would have been interpreted as a revolutionary claim, the promise to rebuild the temple is a messianic declaration. In Jewish literature there was an expectation that the Messiah would establish a new and transformed temple for authentic worship. In this way Mark describes how the death and resurrection of Jesus will be the true destruction and renewal of the temple. His destruction and triumph will be the new order of true worship.

The failure of the witnesses to bring a sustainable charge against Jesus leads the high priest to interrogate Jesus himself. The trial reaches its climax as he asks Jesus, "Are you the Messiah, the Son of the Blessed One?" (verse 61). The response of Jesus is immediate: "I am." This brings together the two central titles of Jesus' identity for Mark's gospel: Christ and Son of God (1:1). His true identity, which has remained hidden and misunderstood by his followers throughout the gospel, now comes to be fully revealed in his passion. Jesus would not let his identity be proclaimed in his moments of triumph. It is only as he is clearly shown to be the Suffering Servant that he can be fully understood. Only now in his weakest moment, bound as a prisoner, betrayed with a kiss, abandoned by his friends, does Jesus allow his fullest titles to be acclaimed unreservedly.

Jesus continues his reply to the high priest with a prophecy of his own triumph. He combines two Scripture texts which he had previously invoked: Daniel 7:13, which speaks of a triumphant figure in human form coming with the clouds of heaven, and Psalm 110:1, in which the king is addressed by God, "Sit at my right hand." This exultant power of Jesus can only be revealed and properly understood in the context of his giving his life through the cross.

In response to Jesus' self-revelation, the high priest dramatically tears his garment and labels the words of Jesus as blasphemy. This is just the kind of self-incrimination the high priest is seeking. With no more need of witnesses, the Sanhedrin unanimously and unhesitatingly condemns Jesus as deserving to die. The scene ends as they mock and beat Jesus as a false prophet, while ironically the prophecies of Jesus continue being fulfilled with the denial of Peter in the courtyard.

Reflection and discussion

• In what sense is the testimony in verse 58 true and in what sense is it false?

• Why did Jesus now boldly admit he is the Messiah and Son of God when he had previously forbidden those titles to be used of him?

• Why is the self-revelation of Jesus described as blasphemy by the high priest? Why is Jesus condemned as deserving to die?

Prayer

Messiah and Son of God, help me to bear witness to you in word and deed. Give me the faith to speak about you to those who need you and to remain true to you in times of trial.

Then Peter remembered that Jesus had said to him,
"Before the cock crows twice, you will deny me three times."
Mark 14:72

Peter Denies Jesus
Three Times

MARK 14:66–72 ⁶⁶*While Peter was below in the courtyard, one of the servant-girls of the high priest came by.* ⁶⁷*When she saw Peter warming himself, she stared at him and said, "You also were with Jesus, the man from Nazareth."* ⁶⁸*But he denied it, saying, "I do not know or understand what you are talking about." And he went out into the forecourt. Then the cock crowed.* ⁶⁹*And the servant-girl, on seeing him, began again to say to the bystanders, "This man is one of them."* ⁷⁰*But again he denied it. Then after a little while the bystanders again said to Peter, "Certainly you are one of them; for you are a Galilean."* ⁷¹*But he began to curse, and he swore an oath, "I do not know this man you are talking about."* ⁷²*At that moment the cock crowed for the second time. Then Peter remembered that Jesus had said to him, "Before the cock crows twice, you will deny me three times." And he broke down and wept.*

Mark picks up the story of Peter, who is in the courtyard while Jesus is under trial by the Sanhedrin. The two scenes form a sharp contrast. As Jesus boldly professes his identity before the highest religious authorities, Peter cowardly denies knowing Jesus. Peter, who a few hours before had proclaimed, "Even though I must die with you, I will not deny you," now denies Jesus before a simple servant girl and a few bystanders. Peter, who has not yet understood or accepted the necessity of the cross, crumbles under his first challenge and cowers in fear and denial.

Like Jesus, Peter is confronted by witnesses. The accusation made against him is that he was "with Jesus" (verse 67), a phrase that expresses the bond between Jesus and his disciples. It is Peter's relationship with Jesus, a bond that had been the meaning of Peter's life, which he denies in his moment of trial.

The drama builds in intensity as Peter's threefold denial gradually escalates to a powerful climax. First, when the servant girl recognizes Peter in the light of the fire and states that he was with Jesus, Peter replies that he does not know what the servant girl is talking about. Peter then edges his way away from the fire and into the forecourt as the cock crows. Second, when the servant girl tells the bystanders that Peter is one of Jesus' disciples, Peter again denies being one of them. Finally, when the bystanders challenge Peter further, stating that he must be a disciple because of his Galilean accent, Peter curses and swears an oath saying, "I do not know this man you are talking about" (verse 71). He cannot even bring himself to say the name of Jesus.

Upon Peter's third denial, the cock crows a second time. The crowing causes Peter to remember Jesus' prediction of his denial and to recall his own rash oath of fidelity. Shattered with the realization of what he has done, Peter weeps tears of remorse and repentance.

Mark makes it clear that Peter's three denials correspond to his threefold failure to keep awake and pray at Gethsemane. In the context of the persecuted church to which the gospel was written, this story of Peter served as a source of hope for the many Christians who denied knowing Jesus in the crisis of persecution or betrayed their discipleship under threat. Many had renounced their faith under oath in order to save the lives of their families and had wept the same bitter tears of remorse. In telling this account of Peter, Mark wanted these Christians to know that even the greatest Christian leader had failed in his discipleship at the most critical hour. Through their failure, they could, like Peter, discover the rich meaning of the cross, the power of resurrection, and the forgiving grace of Jesus.

Reflection and discussion

• What thoughts and feelings might Peter have experienced when he heard the cock crow?

• Have I ever been afraid to admit that I am a disciple of Jesus? What was the source of my fear?

• Why would Mark include this narrative in his gospel, especially if he is writing from Rome under the guidance of Peter?

Prayer

Son of God, forgive me for denying and doubting you. When I experience rejection and suffering, let me look to you as my strength and never let me be separated from you.

SUGGESTIONS FOR FACILITATORS, GROUP SESSION 5

1. Welcome group members and ask if anyone has any questions, announcements, or requests.

2. You may want to pray this prayer as a group:
Eternal Father, as we reflect on the passion accounts, you illuminate our minds and warm our hearts with the fire of divine love that radiates from the heart of Jesus. Guide us as we follow Jesus along the way of the cross, and keep us faithful to him. Help us to recognize our own weaknesses and our ability to deny, betray, and abandon him. Strengthen us with your grace and prepare us for life's most difficult hour, especially as we listen to your word and share the body and blood of Jesus, your Son.

3. Ask one or more of the following questions:
   • What most intrigued you from this week's study?
   • What makes you want to know and understand more of God's word?

4. Discuss lessons 19 through 24. Choose one or more of the questions for reflection and discussion from each lesson to talk over as a group.

5. Ask the group members to name one thing they have most appreciated about the way the group has worked during this Bible study. Ask group members to discuss any changes they might suggest in the way the group works in future studies.

6. Invite group members to complete lessons 25 through 30 on their own during the six days before the next meeting. They should write out their own answers to the questions as preparation for next week's session.

7. Ask group members how the study of the gospel affects their hearing and response to the gospel proclaimed in liturgy.

8. Conclude by praying aloud together the prayer at the end of one of the lessons discussed. You may want to conclude the prayer by asking members to voice prayers of thanksgiving.

They clothed him in a purple cloak; and after twisting some thorns
into a crown, they put it on him. And they began saluting him,
"Hail, King of the Jews!" Mark 15:17–18

Jesus' Trial
before Pontius Pilate

MARK 15:1–20 ¹*As soon as it was morning, the chief priests held a consultation with the elders and scribes and the whole council. They bound Jesus, led him away, and handed him over to Pilate.* ²*Pilate asked him, "Are you the King of the Jews?" He answered him, "You say so."* ³*Then the chief priests accused him of many things.* ⁴*Pilate asked him again, "Have you no answer? See how many charges they bring against you."* ⁵*But Jesus made no further reply, so that Pilate was amazed.*

⁶*Now at the festival he used to release a prisoner for them, anyone for whom they asked.* ⁷*Now a man called Barabbas was in prison with the rebels who had committed murder during the insurrection.* ⁸*So the crowd came and began to ask Pilate to do for them according to his custom.* ⁹*Then he answered them, "Do you want me to release for you the King of the Jews?"* ¹⁰*For he realized that it was out of jealousy that the chief priests had handed him over.* ¹¹*But the chief priests stirred up the crowd to have him release Barabbas for them instead.* ¹²*Pilate spoke to them again, "Then what do you wish me to do with the man you call the King of the Jews?"* ¹³*They shouted back, "Crucify him!"* ¹⁴*Pilate asked them, "Why, what evil has he done?" But they shouted all the more,*

"Crucify him!" [15]*So Pilate, wishing to satisfy the crowd, released Barabbas for them; and after flogging Jesus, he handed him over to be crucified.*

[16]*Then the soldiers led him into the courtyard of the palace (that is, the governor's headquarters); and they called together the whole cohort.* [17]*And they clothed him in a purple cloak; and after twisting some thorns into a crown, they put it on him.* [18]*And they began saluting him, "Hail, King of the Jews!"* [19]*They struck his head with a reed, spat upon him, and knelt down in homage to him.* [20]*After mocking him, they stripped him of the purple cloak and put his own clothes on him. Then they led him out to crucify him.*

Jesus is condemned to death, first by the temple authorities, leaders among the Jews, then by Pilate, a leader among the Gentiles. The gospel symbolically shows that all humanity is implicated in the rejection and crucifixion of Jesus. Jesus is continually "handed over," one to another, when proceeding toward death: Judas handed him over to the chief priests, the priests have handed him over to Pilate (verses 1, 10), and Pilate has handed him over to be crucified (verse 15). The disciples, the Jewish leaders, and the Roman authorities all share in the responsibility for Jesus' death. Again Mark draws the readers into the gospel, because even the crowds share responsibility. Since we continue to sin, their shout, "Crucify him!" is our cry as well.

When Pilate asks Jesus if he is the "king of the Jews," Jesus answers ambiguously. Pilate wants to know if Jesus is a revolutionary, a threat to the authority of the empire. Jesus' response, "You say so," does not fully claim the title of king because of its exalted political connotations, yet does not deny the charge because, as the suffering Messiah, he is a king in a much deeper sense than Pilate could know. The response of Jesus indicates that Pilate has the words right but does not understand the full meaning of his own question. When Jesus makes no further reply to the charges they bring up against him, Pilate is stunned with amazement. He doesn't know what to do with an accused criminal who has not pleaded guilty but who does not assert his innocence or deny the charges against him when questioned.

The custom of releasing a prisoner at Passover seems to have been a concession to the Jews, a conciliatory gesture on the part of the Roman government. Choosing a prisoner to release during the feast of Israel's liberation was meant to cool their revolutionary passions. The choice between Jesus and

Barabbas rests with the crowd, yet they are prompted by the chief priests to call for Barabbas. The name Barabbas literally means "son of the father," providing an ironic choice between Barabbas and the Son of God. The release of Barabbas, followed by the crucifixion of Jesus, expresses how Jesus takes our sins upon himself so that we might go free and live. We are all sons and daughters of the Father, who have been freed and given life by the true Son, Jesus Christ.

The title "King of the Jews" is probably the charge that the chief priests brought against Jesus before Pilate, because the charge of blasphemy, for which Jesus was condemned by the Sanhedrin, would have been of no concern to Pilate. The title is used throughout the remainder of this account (verses 2, 9, 12, 18), and it is the title affixed to the cross on which Jesus dies (verse 26). The title is ambiguous because Jesus is truly the messianic king, not just of the Jews but of all people. Yet he is the suffering king. Jesus is a king who is mocked with a purple cloak, wears a crown of thorns, and is enthroned on a cross. The soldiers' mockery of Jesus as a king reveals the kind of king that Jesus truly is.

Reflection and discussion

• What kind of king is Jesus? What does it mean to belong to his kingdom?

• How would I feel if I were Barabbas—guilty yet set free? In what sense am I Barabbas?

• Why was Pilate amazed? Why was Pilate indecisive?

• What physical, mental, and emotional tortures do the soldiers inflict on Jesus?

• Why is it impossible to blame the death of Jesus on any one group of people?

Prayer

Suffering Messiah, you were handed over to death by crucifixion to satisfy the crowds. Help me to hand over my whole self to you, not to satisfy others but to give glory to you. Reign over my life from your glorious cross.

"He saved others; he cannot save himself.
Let the Messiah, the King of Israel, come down from the cross now,
so that we may see and believe." Mark 15:31–32

The Crucifixion and Mockery of Jesus

MARK 15:21–32 *²¹They compelled a passer-by, who was coming in from the country, to carry his cross; it was Simon of Cyrene, the father of Alexander and Rufus. ²²Then they brought Jesus to the place called Golgotha (which means the place of a skull). ²³And they offered him wine mixed with myrrh; but he did not take it. ²⁴And they crucified him, and divided his clothes among them, casting lots to decide what each should take.*

²⁵It was nine o'clock in the morning when they crucified him. ²⁶The inscription of the charge against him read, "The King of the Jews." ²⁷And with him they crucified two bandits, one on his right and one on his left. ²⁹Those who passed by derided him, shaking their heads and saying, "Aha! You who would destroy the temple and build it in three days, ³⁰save yourself, and come down from the cross!" ³¹In the same way the chief priests, along with the scribes, were also mocking him among themselves and saying, "He saved others; he cannot save himself. ³²Let the Messiah, the King of Israel, come down from the cross now, so that we may see and believe." Those who were crucified with him also taunted him.

Prisoners condemned to crucifixion were often made to carry their own cross, or at least the crossbeam. Apparently Jesus was already weakened by the torture he had endured. Simon of Cyrene, who probably had come to Jerusalem for the Passover, was pressed into service to carry the cross of Jesus. He and his sons, Alexander and Rufus, must have become believers since they are known to the Christian community. Simon, who enters and exits the passion narrative in one verse, reminds us of the nature of discipleship and its cost. According to Jesus, taking up the cross is the mark of true discipleship (8:34).

Crucifixion took place outside the walls of the city, so Jesus would have been led out the city gates. Mark preserves the Aramaic name, Golgotha, for the place of execution, but he translates it for his readers as "the place of a skull." Crucifixion was described by ancient writers as the most cruel and horrifying punishment, and we can imagine the torturous pain that Jesus must have experienced when nailed to the cross and hung there to die. Yet Mark does not dwell on the physical agony; in fact, he describes this climactic event of the gospel in one stark phrase: "They crucified him" (verse 24). Mark's concern, rather, is to help readers understand the meaning of Jesus' death.

This scene of horror, with Jesus affixed to the cross and his royal title fastened to the wood, is Mark's depiction of Jesus fully revealed as the suffering Messiah. The notion that a crucified king could be honored was strange indeed. There had been numerous messianic movements during the century in which Jesus lived, but none of these would-be messiahs had any thought that their cause would come to fruition through their own death. Yet, in a profound sense, Jesus is truly enthroned on the cross because it is from there that he exercises his dominion over evil, sin, and death. He truly reigns from the cross and brings his kingdom into existence through it. He reigns through the act of love in which he gave up his life so that the multitude may live.

The charge against Jesus and the mockery express the true identity of Jesus and his messianic mission. The inscription over the cross, "The King of the Jews," meant as a humiliation, can now be understood in its fullest sense. Those crucified with Jesus, "one on his right and one on his left," become his royal court. When James and John had asked for the places of honor in the kingdom, "one at your right hand and one at your left" (10:37), Jesus promised them instead a share in his passion. Mark again reminds his readers that the places of honor in the kingdom belong to those who share the cross.

The crucified Jesus is cruelly mocked by all levels of society: the passersby, the religious leaders, and the criminals crucified with him. With supreme irony, the mockeries are expressions of Jesus' truest identity: the temple destroyed and rebuilt (verse 29), the one who saves others but not himself (verse 31), and the one who remained on the cross so that others may believe (verse 32). His mission was accomplished on the cross in the most paradoxical form.

Reflection and discussion

• Who has been a Simon of Cyrene for me, helping me carry the cross? How can I be a Simon for others?

• In what sense is Jesus enthroned on the cross? In what sense does he truly reign from the cross?

• In what sense are the three cruel mockeries of Jesus on the cross also expressions of his truest identity?

Prayer

Crucified Savior, you reign from the cross and establish your kingdom in pain. Help me trust that real power and victory are available through the weakness and humility of the cross.

Now when the centurion, who stood facing him, saw that in this way he breathed his last, he said, "Truly this man was God's Son!" Mark 15:39

The Death of Jesus on the Cross

MARK 15:33–39 ³³ *When it was noon, darkness came over the whole land until three in the afternoon.* ³⁴ *At three o'clock Jesus cried out with a loud voice, "Eloi, Eloi, lema sabachthani?" which means, "My God, my God, why have you forsaken me?"* ³⁵ *When some of the bystanders heard it, they said, "Listen, he is calling for Elijah."* ³⁶ *And someone ran, filled a sponge with sour wine, put it on a stick, and gave it to him to drink, saying, "Wait, let us see whether Elijah will come to take him down."* ³⁷ *Then Jesus gave a loud cry and breathed his last.* ³⁸ *And the curtain of the temple was torn in two, from top to bottom.* ³⁹ *Now when the centurion, who stood facing him, saw that in this way he breathed his last, he said, "Truly this man was God's Son!"*

Mark's passion account is organized into patterns of threes: Jesus prays in Gethsemane three times, Peter denies Jesus three times, three groups mock him on the cross, and the crucifixion consists of three periods of three hours each. At the third hour (9 a.m.) Jesus is crucified (verse 25); at the sixth hour (noon) darkness comes over the land (verse 33); and at the ninth hour (3 p.m.) Jesus cries out before his death (verse 34).

110

These hours are marked by starkness, with few details offered of the horrors of crucifixion, the features of which Mark's readers were all too familiar. Abandoned by his disciples, Jesus is alone, in utter isolation. There is no light from the heavens, for darkness has covered the land. The gloominess recalls the darkness that covered the land of Egypt for three days before the first Passover (Exod 10:21–22) and the dreariness prophesied for the day of God's judgment: "I will make the sun go down at noon, and darken the earth in broad daylight" (Amos 8:9).

The anguished cry of Jesus from the cross (verse 34), preserved by Mark in the Aramaic language of Jesus, is taken from the liturgy of Israel (Ps 22:1). Abandoned by all his disciples and darkness covering the sky above him, here in his final moments of life, he feels as if even God has abandoned him. Jesus experiences no comfort, only God-forsakenness, a suffering even worse than his shame, nakedness, and physical torture. At this moment in which Jesus most fully embodies God's love, he feels totally deserted by God. Why? Surely it is because Jesus has totally taken upon himself the sin of the world, a sin that separates us from God. Because of Jesus' complete self-identification with sinners, he dies the most bitter of all deaths in order to save us from such a fate.

The death of Jesus is described with stark simplicity: he gives a loud and wordless cry and lets out his final breath. His death leads to two dramatic consequences which express its saving significance. First, the curtain of the temple is torn in two (verse 38). The curtain refers to the inner veil that hung between the inner sanctuary and the Holy of Holies, beyond which only the high priest could go, and only once a year, on the Day of Atonement. Its rending "from top to bottom" indicates that God has does the tearing, removing the barrier between himself and humanity. Through his saving death, Jesus has opened access to God for all people. The torn curtain portends the end of sacrifice according to the old covenant, since the temple would be replaced by a new temple "not made with hands" (14:58), with Jesus himself as the cornerstone. The second consequence of Jesus' death is the confession by the Roman centurion in charge of Jesus' execution. His words are the fullest expression of Jesus' identity: "Truly this man was God's Son!" In contrast to the mockers who demanded that Jesus come down from the cross so that they may "see and believe" (verse 32), the centurion sees Jesus give up his life on the cross and believes. The faith of this Gentile is the first saving result of Jesus' sacrifice.

Reflection and discussion

• What difference does it make to me that I follow a crucified Messiah? What does the manner of Jesus' death express to me about God's saving will?

• Since Jesus knew many psalms by heart, Mark assumes that the reader will know that he went on to pray the entire Psalm 22 as his final prayer. What does praying this psalm with the heart of Jesus teach me about his final thoughts on the cross?

• What do the two dramatic consequences of Jesus' death on the cross express about the meaning of his death?

Prayer

Crucified Savior, you embraced my suffering and atoned for my sins on the cross. Let me know that you are always with me, even when I feel alone and abandoned.

These used to follow him and provided for him when he was in Galilee; and there were many other women who had come up with him to Jerusalem.

Mark 15:41

The Women at the Cross and at the Tomb

MARK 15:40–47 ⁴⁰*There were also women looking on from a distance; among them were Mary Magdalene, and Mary the mother of James the younger and of Joses, and Salome. ⁴¹These used to follow him and provided for him when he was in Galilee; and there were many other women who had come up with him to Jerusalem.*

⁴²*When evening had come, and since it was the day of Preparation, that is, the day before the sabbath, ⁴³Joseph of Arimathea, a respected member of the council, who was also himself waiting expectantly for the kingdom of God, went boldly to Pilate and asked for the body of Jesus. ⁴⁴Then Pilate wondered if he were already dead; and summoning the centurion, he asked him whether he had been dead for some time. ⁴⁵When he learned from the centurion that he was dead, he granted the body to Joseph. ⁴⁶Then Joseph bought a linen cloth, and taking down the body, wrapped it in the linen cloth, and laid it in a tomb that had been hewn out of the rock. He then rolled a stone against the door of the tomb. ⁴⁷Mary Magdalene and Mary the mother of Joses saw where the body was laid.*

A t the conclusion of the passion, Mark focuses on a group of women who were "looking on from a distance." They were far enough away from the cross so as not to give active assent to what was happening but close enough to be sympathetic witnesses to these climactic events. Their presence during Jesus' dark hours is a stark reminder of the flight of the chosen Twelve at the arrest of Jesus and their glaring absence at the cross.

Although Mark only mentions a few of these women by name, he states that there were "many other women" who had come with Jesus from Galilee. Apparently Jesus had quite a number of female disciples who followed him along the way. The freedom that these women enjoyed, traveling as an itinerant band of disciples, must have seemed extraordinary in the culture of the time. The verbs used to describe the actions of these women indicate that they were true disciples. Mark says they used to "follow" Jesus in Galilee, a word indicating discipleship. He also states that the women "provided" for him, a word that can also mean "served" or "ministered," another indication of genuine discipleship. And finally, Mark states that these women "had come up with him to Jerusalem," referring to their unity with him in the fulfillment of his mission in the way of the cross. Their faithful following and service are models for all future disciples.

Mark tells us that Jesus died on a Friday, "the day of Preparation, that is, the day before the sabbath," a short time after the ninth hour (3 p.m.). Since the Sabbath begins at sundown and since the work of burial is prohibited on the Sabbath, there is little time to obtain permission from Pilate for the body of Jesus, acquire the necessary supplies, and prepare the body for burial. Introduced here for the first time, Joseph of Arimathea hurries to claim and bury the body of Jesus. Joseph purchases a linen cloth, removes Jesus from the cross, cleans his body, closes his eyes, wraps him in the shroud, lays him inside the tomb, and rolls the stone across the entrance. The fearlessness and dedication of Joseph form another strong contrast to the cowardly Twelve. Joseph did what Jesus' closest followers should have done.

Those who were faithful to the end were not those we would expect. The centurion, the women, Joseph of Arimathea—these represent what the church would be. Women and men, Jews and Gentiles, together form the Christian community, called to share the humble, loving, self-giving life of Jesus. This community formed at the cross must have felt that their beloved Jesus was gone forever. The linen cloth, the rock-hewn tomb, the heavy stone—all made his death seem so final. Jesus was crucified, died, and was buried. If that were the end, the gospel would not be good news but a tragedy. The finality of this scene only prepares us for the empty tomb and the announcement that Jesus has been raised.

Reflection and discussion

• How does Mark contrast the women of Galilee with the twelve male disciples of Jesus? How do these women demonstrate the most important characteristics of discipleship?

• Why does Mark contrast Joseph and the women with the Twelve? What makes some people courageous and others cowardly in the face of crisis?

• Imagine Joseph of Arimathea tending to the burial details for the body of Jesus. How might Joseph have felt during each of these actions between the cross and the tomb?

Prayer

Merciful Jesus, you formed your church at the foot of the cross, giving your saving grace to men and women, Jews and Gentiles, who honor you. Help me to imitate the faith, hope, and love of the centurion, the women, and Joseph of Arimathea as I look upon your cross.

"You are looking for Jesus of Nazareth, who was crucified. He has been raised; he is not here. Look, there is the place they laid him." Mark 16:6

The Proclamation of Jesus' Resurrection

MARK 16:1–8 ¹*When the sabbath was over, Mary Magdalene, and Mary the mother of James, and Salome bought spices, so that they might go and anoint him. ²And very early on the first day of the week, when the sun had risen, they went to the tomb. ³They had been saying to one another, "Who will roll away the stone for us from the entrance to the tomb?" ⁴When they looked up, they saw that the stone, which was very large, had already been rolled back. ⁵As they entered the tomb, they saw a young man, dressed in a white robe, sitting on the right side; and they were alarmed. ⁶But he said to them, "Do not be alarmed; you are looking for Jesus of Nazareth, who was crucified. He has been raised; he is not here. Look, there is the place they laid him. ⁷But go, tell his disciples and Peter that he is going ahead of you to Galilee; there you will see him, just as he told you." ⁸So they went out and fled from the tomb, for terror and amazement had seized them; and they said nothing to anyone, for they were afraid.*

This climactic announcement of Christ's resurrection is the end of Mark's gospel. The earliest manuscripts of the gospel end with verse 8, leaving the gospel radically open-ended. Later writers added a variety of endings in order to "complete" Mark's presentation and to include the church's tradition of resurrection appearances. However, since Mark concludes his account of the good news with the women fleeing the tomb, we must try to understand why Mark would leave his gospel with this sense of incompleteness.

The Sabbath, the last day of the week, has ended, and the women discover the empty tomb on Sunday morning, "very early on the first day of the week, when the sun had risen." Genesis depicts the first day of the week as the beginning of God's creation, and Mark describes the resurrection as the beginning of God's new creation. The "first day of the week," soon called "the Lord's day," is the day when the early Christians met for eucharistic worship to celebrate God's mighty act of raising Jesus from the dead.

Clearly and concisely, Mark relates the fact of the empty tomb and the reason for its emptiness. The huge stone rolled away from the entrance of the tomb gives the first hint that the tomb is empty. The young man dressed in white is the interpreting angel. The encounter is described in the familiar pattern of angelic messages: the angel appears, the receivers are fearful, the angel tells them not to fear and gives the explanation, and the hearers receive a commission. The messenger's explanation for the empty tomb is startling: "He has been raised." The message brings a dramatic reversal to the passion account which seemed to end with the abandonment and the tragic death of Jesus. The messenger's commission to the women, to go and tell the disciples that Jesus is going ahead of them to Galilee where they will see him, offers a fresh beginning to the lives of those who have fled in denial and desertion. In that commission lies the promise of forgiveness and a renewed calling to follow him.

The end of Mark's gospel can be rightly called a cliffhanger. It ends quite abruptly: "They went out and fled from the tomb, for terror and amazement had seized them; and they said nothing to anyone, for they were afraid." Throughout his gospel Mark has demonstrated the response of the disciples as misunderstanding, fear, failure, and flight. He has brought his readers into the experience of the original disciples to hear Jesus' astonishing claims and startling words that overturn mere human ways of thinking. Again, Mark brings his readers into the story with his final verse. We too are brought to the empty tomb to hear the announcement of Jesus' victory over death. How are we going to respond?

Mark certainly knew the accounts of Jesus resurrection appearances and could have added them here. But Mark wanted to put the emphasis elsewhere. Writing in Rome to teach people in the next generation how to be disciples, Mark chooses to leave his gospel without a conclusion. The resurrection is not the end of the gospel, but only the beginning. Jesus has gone ahead of his disciples where he will meet them where they began. Mark leaves his account incomplete because the good news of Jesus is incomplete. Our problem is that we have heard the story of Jesus so often that we fail to react because we think we know how it ends. But that is Mark's point; we don't know how it will end. Mark's gospel is incomplete and open-ended, to be completed with our own lives recreated by God in the light of the risen Christ. We are invited to accept in faith the announcement of his resurrection and to continue the story in every age.

Reflection and discussion

• What is the significance in the fact that Christ rose on the first day of the week?

• Why did Mark choose not to include the appearances of the risen Jesus as in the other three gospels?

• What is Mark trying to communicate to me with the abrupt and incomplete ending to his gospel?

Prayer

Risen Lord, you have defeated the powers of sin and death with your saving death and glorious resurrection. Take away my insecurities and help me to trust in your victory. Make me ready to follow you wherever you lead.

And they went out and proclaimed the good news everywhere, while the Lord worked with them and confirmed the message by the signs that accompanied it. Mark 16:20

The Longer Ending to Mark's Gospel

MARK 16:9–20 ⁹*Now after he rose early on the first day of the week, he appeared first to Mary Magdalene, from whom he had cast out seven demons.* ¹⁰*She went out and told those who had been with him, while they were mourning and weeping.* ¹¹*But when they heard that he was alive and had been seen by her, they would not believe it.*

¹²*After this he appeared in another form to two of them, as they were walking into the country.* ¹³*And they went back and told the rest, but they did not believe them.*

¹⁴*Later he appeared to the eleven themselves as they were sitting at the table; and he upbraided them for their lack of faith and stubbornness, because they had not believed those who saw him after he had risen.* ¹⁵*And he said to them, "Go into all the world and proclaim the good news to the whole creation.* ¹⁶*The one who believes and is baptized will be saved; but the one who does not believe will be condemned.* ¹⁷*And these signs will accompany those who believe: by using my name they will cast out demons; they will speak in new tongues;* ¹⁸*they will pick up snakes in their hands, and if they drink any deadly thing, it will not hurt them; they will lay their hands on the sick, and they will recover."*

[19]*So then the Lord Jesus, after he had spoken to them, was taken up into heaven and sat down at the right hand of God.* [20]*And they went out and proclaimed the good news everywhere, while the Lord worked with them and confirmed the message by the signs that accompanied it.*

The earliest manuscripts of Mark's gospel end with verse 8, though other writers added endings to the gospel because they assumed that Mark was unable to finish his gospel or that the ending had been lost. These various endings, the longest of which is contained in these final verses of the gospel, are compiled summaries of several accounts of Jesus' resurrection appearances from the other gospels. The unique vocabulary and diverse style of these endings indicate that they were written by a different author at a later time. The church, however, has accepted this addendum to Mark's gospel as a part of inspired Scripture since this ending is part of the gospel's final edited form.

The first appearance to Mary Magdalene is consistent with the other gospels, but when she communicates the news that Jesus is alive to the others, they do not believe her. The next appearance summarizes the appearance of Jesus to two disciples on the road to Emmaus from Luke's gospel. Again, the others do not believe them. When Jesus appears to the eleven at table, reminiscent of the account in Luke and John, he rebukes them for their refusal to believe his witnesses. Then Jesus commissions them with the same charge that concludes the gospel of Matthew: "Go into all the world and proclaim the good news to the whole creation" (verse 15). The good news is no longer limited to the people of Israel, but it is destined for the whole world, Jews and Gentiles alike. The proclaimed word is accompanied by signs and wonders, and those who believe in Jesus and accept baptism are welcomed into the community of salvation.

This longer addendum concludes with an account of Jesus' ascension in which Jesus is called "the Lord," a declaration of his divine sovereignty. In response, the disciples "went out and proclaimed the good news everywhere, while the Lord worked with them." Though Jesus is enthroned in heaven, he still works with his disciples on earth. He remains present and powerfully at work in the church throughout the ages.

The proclamation of the good news, which began Mark's gospel, now concludes this ending. Living that good news through struggle, misunderstanding, joy, loyalty, suffering, death, and resurrection is what following Jesus is all about. This proclamation of the gospel by Jesus is now the task for the whole church: "The time is fulfilled, and the kingdom of God has come near; repent, and believe in the good news" (1:15).

Reflection and discussion

• In what ways do I experience the presence and the absence of Jesus?

• What would my life be like if I truly believed with all my heart that Jesus is risen and alive?

• What is the primary message I want to remember from my study of Mark's gospel?

Prayer

Lord Jesus, you are alive and risen. Open my eyes to see your presence around me; open my mouth to speak the good news. Empower me to be your witness, and assure me that you work with me through the power of your Spirit.

SUGGESTIONS FOR FACILITATORS, GROUP SESSION 6

1. Welcome group members and make any final announcements or requests.

2. You may want to pray this prayer as a group:

Father of our Lord Jesus Christ, you have given us the inspired words of the gospel according to Mark so that we may come to know Jesus and to understand what it means to follow him. When he is seen as the Suffering Servant at the cross, we understand the purpose of his mission most clearly. At the moment of his deepest humiliation, his exalted status as Messiah, King of Israel, Builder of the Temple, and Son of God comes to light in its truest meaning. Through his resurrection, may we take up the mission of discipleship to bring the gospel of healing and forgiveness to our broken world.

3. Ask one or more of the following questions:
   - How has this study of Mark's gospel enriched your life?
   - In what way has this study challenged you the most?

4. Discuss lessons 25 through 30. Choose one or more of the questions for reflection and discussion from each lesson to discuss as a group.

5. Ask the group if they would like to study another in the Threshold Bible Study series. Discuss the topic and dates, and make a decision among those interested. Ask the group members to suggest people they would like to invite to participate in the next study series.

6. Ask the group to discuss the insights that stand out most from this study over the past six weeks.

7. Conclude by praying aloud the following prayer or another of your own choosing:

Holy Spirit of the living God, you inspired the writers of Scripture and you have guided our study during these weeks. Continue to deepen our love for the word of God in the holy gospels, and draw us more deeply into the heart of Jesus. We thank you for the confident hope you have placed within us and the gifts which build up the church. Through this study, lead us to worship and witness more fully and fervently, and bless us now and always with the fire of your love.

THE **GOSPEL OF MARK** IN THE SUNDAY LECTIONARY

KEY: **Reading** Sunday or feast *(Lectionary #-Cycle)*

Mark 1:1-8
2nd Sunday of Advent *(5-B)*

Mark 1:7-11
Sunday after Epiphany:
Baptism of the Lord *(21-B)*

Mark 1:12-15
1st Sunday of Lent *(23-B)*

Mark 1:14-20
3rd Sunday in Ordinary Time
(68-B)

Mark 1:21-28
4th Sunday in Ordinary Time
(71-B)

Mark 1:29-39
5th Sunday in Ordinary Time
(74-B)

Mark 1:40-45
6th Sunday in Ordinary Time
(77-B)

Mark 2:1-12
7th Sunday in Ordinary Time
(80-B)

Mark 2:18-22
8th Sunday in Ordinary Time
(83-B)

Mark 2:23—3:6 or 2:23-28
9th Sunday in Ordinary Time
(86-B)

Mark 3:20-35
10th Sunday in Ordinary Time
(89-B)

Mark 4:26-34
11th Sunday in Ordinary Time
(92-B)

Mark 4:35-41
12th Sunday in Ordinary Time
(95-B)

Mark 5:21-43 or 5:21-24, 35-43
13th Sunday in Ordinary Time
(98-B)

Mark 6:1-6
14th Sunday in Ordinary Time
(101-B)

Mark 6:7-13
15th Sunday in Ordinary Time
(104-B)

Mark 6:30-34
16th Sunday in Ordinary Time
(107-B)

Mark 7:1-8, 14-15, 21-23
22nd Sunday in Ordinary Time
(125-B)

Mark 7:31-37
23rd Sunday in Ordinary Time
(128-B)

Mark 8:27-35
24th Sunday in Ordinary Time
(131-B)

Mark 9:2-10
2nd Sunday of Lent *(26-B)*

Mark 9:30-37
25th Sunday in Ordinary Time
(134-B)

Mark 9:38-43, 45, 47-48
26th Sunday in Ordinary Time
(137-B)

Mark 10:2-16 or 10:2-12
27th Sunday in Ordinary Time
(140-B)

Mark 10:17-30 or 10:17-27
28th Sunday in Ordinary Time
(143-B)

Mark 10:35-45 or 10:42-45
29th Sunday in Ordinary Time
(146-B)

Mark 10:46-52
30th Sunday in Ordinary Time
(149-B)

Mark 11:1-10
Palm Sunday: Procession
of Palms (opt. 1) *(37-B)*

Mark 12:28b-34
31st Sunday in Ordinary Time
(152-B)

Mark 12:38-44 or 12:41-44
32nd Sunday in Ordinary Time
(155-B)

Mark 13:24-32
33rd Sunday in Ordinary Time
(158-B)

Mark 13:33-37
1st Sunday of Advent *(2-B)*

**Mark 14:1—15:47
or 15:1-39**
Palm Sunday Mass *(38-B)*

Mark 14:12-16, 22-26
Sunday after Trinity Sun: Body
& Blood of Christ *(168-B)*

Mark 16:1-7
Easter Vigil *(41-B)*

Mark 16:15-20
Ascension of the Lord *(58-B)*

Ordering Additional Studies

To check availability or for a description
of each study, visit our website at
www.ThresholdBibleStudy.com
or call us at **1-800-321-0411**

TWENTY THIRD 23rd PUBLICATIONS